PLANNING FOR RETIREMENT

RELAX, IT'S PLAYTIME!

7 DECISIVE STEPS YOU CAN TAKE NOW AND ELIMINATE STRESS IN PLANNING FOR RETIREMENT

PHILIP B PALLETTE

CONTENTS

INTRODUCTION

"Retirement: It's nice to get out of the rat race, but you have to learn to get along with less cheese."

— **GENE PERRET**

You might wonder why you have a book on retirement in your hand. You are not even near retirement age, or maybe you are just starting your career. You might have even retired and don't know how to navigate your plans. This book answers all your questions about retirement, exactly the same answers James wasn't aware of before running out of the road.

James, an accountant, had a booming career. He journeyed in and out of the buildings on Wall Street. Having known so much about finance, James began investing and saving hugely from his salary until he had an accident that forced him to early retirement. This accident was so severe that James had little to nothing left by the time he was done with treatment. While still actively working, James didn't think much about what to do when he retired. If James had known that he would be retiring early, he might have been strategic and proactive in his planning.

Although you may not be like James or as wealthy as he was, it's always best to start planning retirement as early as possible. So many employees today make countless mistakes about retirement, and one of the most prevalent is waiting until they are close to retiring before considering a retirement investment.

From the story above, you may wonder what the difference between financial plans and retirement plans is. Many investors believe that every dollar you invest has an ultimate goal: the future. However, you may not have a plan for what you want to do after retirement and may wonder if this future prosperity relates to you. But the thoughts about what to expect after retirement shouldn't weigh you down. You should be more concerned about how your current actions will help you have a fulfilling retirement.

IT IS NEVER TOO LATE.

I understand you have goals: saving for a new car for the family, moving to a bigger house, or dreaming of sipping coconut juice in a beach house. You may also have thought of the ability to afford your kids' college fees, or maybe you are saving for a bigger home. All these goals are near goals, and your thoughts should focus more on your retirement.

You may be young, but it is never too early to begin planning for your retirement. Rather than waiting until you receive your retirement check to begin preparing, you should start now. Why? So, you don't become dependent on others after being self-sufficient your whole professional life.

Let's assume that retirement is a huge mountain you want to climb. A tent house at the edge of this mountain gives you the privilege of seeing the rest of the world from a high cliff. What will you need to climb the mountain? A good pair of shoes, enough water to sustain you, a guide, and maybe little or no load. With this, you can climb the mountain with ease, or maybe not.

As seen in the analogy, the pair of shoes is money, and all other material needs are an investment, and that's where the practical guide, ***Financial Planning for Retirement,*** comes in.

Financial Planning for Retirement will show the retirement planning options that exist. With my years of expertise in Financial Retirement Planning (FPR), I will carefully take you through the necessary options. You'll also get step-by-step strategies to plan for your retirement. This guide will not only show you how to plan your retirement financially but also make you see that it is not too late or too early to start planning.

Even if you do not have a substantial sum of money set aside for your old age, you can rely on the retirement benefits your firm must provide. In most countries, companies are required by law to enroll their employees in adequate retirement programs that correspond with their salaries. This means the retirement structure won't overlook you in your old age.

Just like any other type of financial planning, retirement planning is to assess what your potential sources of income and expenditures are likely to be. This will likely be only an estimate and a deciding factor of how far you are from retiring. However, whether you are nearing or have already retired, it is not too late to start planning your financial future, making the process easier.

Financial Planning for Retirement explains in detail how you can manage, earn, grow, and protect your money. You will also know the steps to set financial goals. You may be saving for something in the near future, but this book will show you what it means to have long-term goals and how you can have them too.

After finishing this book, you will also see the types of retirement savings programs and how you can choose for yourself. No matter your age or health status, this book will guide you through the ways to a happy retirement.

WHY DID I WRITE THIS BOOK?

As an acknowledged expert in Financial Planning for Retirement (FPR) who has invested as much as 35 years studying this aspect extensively, I became passionate about helping others avoid some of the costly mistakes in retirement planning. I've gone through the various stages of retirement personally and helped so many people find solutions to their retirement planning. During this time, I taught many people strategies that had worked for me and are still working for people in various fields, hence my passion for sharing these practical and personal nuggets.

Helping you to achieve retirement confidence and well-being matters deeply to me because the guide, ***Financial Planning for Retirement***, is the explanation that allowed me to organize and recognize appropriate action in time for me to achieve post-retirement contentment. As you read through the pages of this book, you will see some of the life decisions you must make to have a fulfilling retirement.

This guide is structured in a way that resonates with everyone regardless of how young you are. So, if you are still very young, you don't have to wait till you are close to retirement before reading this book. And if you are already in retirement, now is the time to make better plans using this practical guide.

So, why not follow me to see the tried-and-true modern and strategic ways of planning for your retirement?

Happy reading!

1

OUR CAPACITY TO PLAN AND SAVE

How much you enjoy your retirement depends on your capacity to plan and save. Just like a computer, garbage in is equal to garbage out. Many people make the costly mistake of ignoring the place of financial planning for their retirement. Most of them greatly regret their actions when they are old, and unfortunately, it's mostly too late. Without proper financial planning, your savings will run out before you do, leaving you without the money you need to live off of when you stop working. This can be frustrating and embarrassing,

The place of financial planning for your retirement cannot be overemphasized. Financial planning for retirement is an essential part of setting up your finances for success in the future. With it, you can make better decisions about your finances and how you want to spend your time. In addition, it helps you ensure that you're saving enough money in case of emergencies, as well as providing the extra income you'll need to live comfortably in retirement.

Arguably, retirement is one of the biggest expenses you will face in your lifetime—so it makes sense to take steps now to make sure you're prepared. This chapter provides a detailed yet simple insight into how to save and plan for your future.

5 PILLARS OF FINANCIAL WELLNESS

Every decision you make about your money has an impact on your financial wellness. Maintaining one's financial health may be challenging. However, these five pillars of financial wellness can help you maintain your finances.

Managing Money

Managing your money can come in several ways. The practices may not be the same because we have different spending habits; however, the principles are the same. To manage your funds successfully, you should consider doing these things:

Budgeting: Living on a budget can prevent you from spending extravagantly.

Tracking your spending: When you track your spending, you will be able to know how much you are spending.

Paying off debt: When you pay off your debt, you will be free to afford the resources and lifestyle you desire.

Saving: Saving your monetary resources allows you to afford life purchases like cars and homes.

Earn Money

Earning is another important aspect of financial wellness. There are diverse ways to sustainably and consistently make money. Note the word sustainability and consistently. You will find it difficult to manage your funds when you earn randomly. The two major ways to earn are through:

Passive income: Earning through means where you don't have to be physically involved. An example is an income from real estate.

Active income: Here, your presence is involved in the earning process. For example, you can be involved in offering a service or selling a product.

Passive and active income have their advantages and disadvantages. Your decision depends on how you get your funds and if the earnings can be consistent, maybe week over week or month over month.

Grow Your Money

If you don't grow your money, you might be revolving around a circle in your finance without any significant change. Many grow their money by saving and investing.

For instance, you can save a percentage of your income every payday. You can then proceed to invest what you have saved either through dividend stocks, retirement accounts, etc.

There are many tips to help you grow your money; below are the most important ones:

- Commitment
- Consistency
- Intentionality

Smart Borrowing

Borrowing allows you to take advantage of some forms of finance like credit and can be beneficial when you establish credit and credible financial history. To borrow smartly, you have to stop overspending as you build up a credible payment history.

To achieve this:

- Borrow only what you can pay back.
- Pay your debt before the due date.
- Have few credit lines.
- Don't close outstanding credit lines.

Borrowing can also include taking loans like home or auto loans to build credit. Although borrowing is a responsibility, in the long run, it can yield great rewards for your financial well-being.

Protect Your Funds

Protecting your money is a serious issue; you should not take it for granted. Insurance is a good way to protect your assets and protect your future. Insurance gives you rest and peace of mind because you know that you have protection for your financial loss.

Other ways to protect your money are:

- Have a strong password for your financial account.
- Deal with only verified banking services.
- Don't log into your personal financial account on another person's computer.

FIVE PILLARS FOR A SUCCESSFUL RETIREMENT PLAN

Learning about the five pillars of your financial wellness is important to learn how to have a successful retirement. These pillars, just like the previous ones, can have different approaches for different people, but the principles are the same for those who want peace of mind when they retire.

Income Planning

You will not like to be in a position to make drastic changes to your lifestyle because the transition will be difficult and expensive. But, on the other hand, you also don't want to be in the position of not having enough money to support yourself when you're retired—that would be a terrible way to start your life post-work. So, it is vital to find a balance between making sure you have enough income while also ensuring your lifestyle isn't too different from what it was while working. And that is why income planning is a crucial part of your financial future.

Income planning is a process you and your financial advisor go through to determine the exact amount you need to make to live comfortably for the rest of your life. You should consider different factors, including your current lifestyle and what kind of retirement benefits you expect to receive.

Retirement plans come in two folds: traditional and Roth IRAs.

The difference between the two is simple. With traditional IRAs, you are expected to be taxed whenever you make a withdrawal. But with the Roth IRAs, withdrawals are tax-free.

When determining how much income you'll need in retirement, it's important to consider all of these factors:

- Your age and health status.
- Your savings rate.
- The length of time you expect to live.

Investment Planning

Retirement planning is a complicated process, and it can be hard to get it right. In order to help you make the best decisions, here are some tips to help you invest for retirement.

First, start by deciding what kind of retirement you want. Do you want to live off of savings? Or do you want to travel around the world? If so, then start making plans for how much money will be necessary for that lifestyle. Once you know what kind of life you want in retirement, decide whether or not investing is right for you.

If investing is the best thing for you, then it's time to think about where and how much money should be invested. You should base your decision on some factors, including your age, risk tolerance level, and how long you'll be investing. An important thing to note when investing is that the market tends to go up and down over time. This means your investments may grow, decline, or even disappear altogether. Investing in a diversified portfolio that includes stocks, bonds, and other assets (such as real estate) is very important.

Tax Planning

When you're planning for retirement, tax planning is a crucial part of the process. When you get older and begin to think about how much money you'll need to save for your golden years, it's easy to get caught up in the excitement of planning and forget that the tax implications of your financial decisions can be just as important. Tax planning for retirement can help you avoid paying unnecessary taxes on investments and ensure your savings are protected from inflation over time. Here are some tips for tax planning for retirement:

– Make sure you contribute at least enough money into an IRA or 401(k) plan to cover all your eligible expenses during retirement. If necessary, increase your contribution amount during high-income years until it covers all eligible expenses.

– Make sure that any taxable investments have a good track record (i.e., don't invest in companies with poor reputations). This is especially true if these types of investments don't pay dividends or interest regularly; instead, put them into low-cost index funds that track broad market indexes such as the S&P 500 Index (or its equivalent).

– You may also want to keep investment accounts separate from each other so that they don't get taxed twice when it comes time to withdraw money or make investments with them. If you diversify investments and want to see how much each one is worth at any given point in time, you can use tax software to track them all in one place.

Health Care Planning

You might have heard the term "retirement" and thought, "Oh, that's just when you stop working." But it's much more than that—it's when you start to plan for your health care needs as you age. As you grow older, you will likely need more medical attention, which is why you need to plan for your health care before retirement.

Health care planning is a process of identifying and managing your health care needs, whether you're living alone or with your family. This includes ensuring you have the right kind of coverage, that you are getting the right care, and that you are paying for it in a way that will allow you to continue living comfortably.

It's important to plan ahead so that you're not faced with unexpected medical bills when they're already overwhelming. Because as you age, your health care needs might change in a number of ways:

- You may need more preventive care than you did when you were younger.
- You may have special needs for long-term care or nursing home care.
- You may want to transition from Medicare to Medicaid or from one type of insurance plan to another.
- Your doctor might recommend changing medications or seeking treatment for conditions that cause pain or limit mobility.

Legacy Planning

People easily ponder their life in retirement. However, they may not have any idea where to start or what to do next.

Legacy Planning can help you get started on the path toward a secure life for your family. Legacy planning is the process of identifying and creating an estate plan that will ensure your family's financial security after your death. However, you don't have to have a formal estate plan or even have one at all; set up a plan so that the distribution of your assets can be handled efficiently and effectively. The first step in legacy planning is identifying who will inherit your property and how they will get it. This includes identifying what property you own as well as who owns any other property (such as life insurance or retirement accounts).

Once you have identified who inherits what, it's time to decide on how they'll get it. For example, if you want them to receive cash instead of property, you may want to consider setting up a revocable trust instead of giving them money outright. Your beneficiaries may also want to set up their retirement accounts (IRA) or a 401(k) account if possible—and remember that if they're working full time at least until age 67 and older, then they may qualify for Roth IRAs too!

NARRATIVE FINANCIAL THERAPY

Narrative Financial Therapy is a form of psychotherapy that integrates a financial planning approach with therapeutic theory. Narrative therapy uses stories and narratives to identify, understand and deal with clients' past, present, and future lives.

Narrative Financial Therapy is based on the idea that our beliefs about ourselves and our world influence how we act in the world. The therapist helps clients change their beliefs by helping them understand their stories; this helps clients create new stories that they can use to be more effective in their lives.

Narrative Financial Therapy: "Integrating a Financial Planning Approach with Therapeutic Theory

Narrative Financial Therapy (NFT) is a new approach to therapy that integrates a financial planning approach with the tenets of narrative therapy. This article will discuss how NFT differs from traditional approaches and how it can be used to help clients with various issues.

Narrative therapy was first developed in the early 1970s by psychiatrist David Storr, who believed that people were more fully human when they were able to express their thoughts and feelings. Narratives can be anything from stories about your life to what you did last night or how you feel about something right now.

The goal of NFT is to help people tell their stories through writing, artwork, or even video recordings. The therapist then helps the client see connections between their story and other parts of their life, including their finances.

Although psychiatrists developed NFT, it's not limited to those with mental health concerns; many therapists use it for clients dealing with addiction or personality disorders and business owners trying to make business decisions.

Narrative financial therapy is a form of therapy that integrates a financial planning approach with therapeutic theory. Narrative financial therapy is based on the understanding that people develop their narratives about their lives, which may be positive or negative. Narrative financial therapy aims to help clients develop positive narratives about their lives and make those narratives more consistent with reality.

NFT addresses the root of problems by helping clients develop new ways of thinking about themselves and their problems. In particular, the treatment helps clients identify their core values, goals, and purpose in life (their "why"). This helps them see opportunities they may have missed and new ways to think about themselves and their lives.

The most important step in narrative financial therapy is helping clients develop an accurate picture of what they have accomplished in life so far. Clients are asked to write down as many accomplishments as they can think of by using whatever method works best for them (for example, listing accomplishments from memory). This exercise helps clients see how much they have achieved so far, allowing them to identify areas for improvement in other areas of their lives. NFT is an integrative approach to financial problems that combines cognitive-behavioral therapy (CBT) and narrative therapy. NFT focuses on helping clients develop a more positive view of themselves and their ability to deal with financial issues. The treatment helps clients understand how their finances affect their lives and how to manage those finances more positively.

Narrative therapy focuses on the client's story, examining the past and present about their life circumstances; it also looks at solutions they may have missed or are not yet aware of. Clients who use narrative therapy gain a deeper understanding of their circumstances and a way to express repressed emotions.

The Certified Financial Planner Board of Standards, Inc.'s six-step financial planning process is included in the proposed model (CFP Board, 2013). The Certified Financial Planner Board is in charge of awarding the CFP designation and upholding moral standards for CFP practitioners. The sequential steps in the six-step process are as follows:

1. Identify the client-planner relationship and define it.
2. Compile client data and talk about objectives.
3. Examine and assess the financial situation of the client.
4. Construct and deliver a financial plan.
5. Put the financial plan into action.
6. Keep an eye on the budget.

Incorporate integrative therapies – How Financial Therapy Can Lead to a Brighter Financial Future.

Financial Therapy's Development

In 2008, financial professionals, mental health professionals, educators, and researchers came together to discuss the idea of financial therapy. The Financial Therapy Association (FTA) received official nonprofit status eleven months later. Since then, the FTA has worked to spread its vision of integrating well-cognitive, emotional, behavioral, relational, and financial facets.

The approaches to financial therapy can vary because there are various ways that mental health and finance professionals can work together. In addition, there are numerous other reasons why someone might require financial therapy. However, it usually involves behavioral problems.

The first step to finding a financial therapist is to know whether or not you need one. Financial therapists are trained in the diagnosis and treatment of financial issues. There are resources to help you with questions about your finances. The best way to know if you need a financial therapist is to talk with someone who can help.

Financial therapists can provide:

- Help with budgeting.
- Help with how to pay bills on time.

- Help with how much money you have saved for retirement.
- Advice on managing debt and credit cards.

If you're feeling stressed, anxious, or overwhelmed by your finances, it might be time to seek financial therapy. Financial therapy can help people with low credit scores and limited access to credit repair services.

Financial therapy includes the following:

Financial therapists don't have licenses or other credentials that qualify them as experts in the field. But they often work with licensed financial advisors, who provide services under a professional license.

Financial therapists may be licensed to practice in certain states, but most states do not provide supervision and oversight of the treatment process. A common model for providing these services is for a licensed professional to oversee a group of therapists working one-on-one with clients. Financial therapists typically work one-on-one with clients and are not certified as social workers or psychologists. However, some states require these professionals to obtain state licenses before practicing.

Financial Therapy for Dealing with Money and Emotions

Financial therapy is a psychotherapy that helps people resolve their finances, understand their money issues, and make better financial decisions. If you feel overwhelmed by the demands on your time and energy due to your finances, financial therapy can help. You can think of the connection between money and emotions as a cycle. Financial difficulties can have a detrimental effect on your mental well-being. For instance, stress and depression can be brought on by excessive debt. Thirty-one percent of Americans in debt claim to worry about it frequently, while 25 percent worry about it right before bed!

Your mental health may impact finances. For example, financial stress and problems with money can be caused by poor mental health. You might then make poor financial decisions as a result, which would make your anxiety even worse.

People really care about their financial situation and how much money they have. Their thoughts, feelings, and emotions may positively or negatively impact their financial decisions. It can be harmful not to comprehend this relationship cycle and to deal with financial issues and weaknesses improperly. A financial therapist can be useful in this situation. The actions listed below can help you decide whether consulting with a financial therapist would benefit you by outlining what they offer:

1. Recognize the negative habits

A financial therapist may identify problematic behaviors as part of their work. Then, they assist clients in recognizing these behaviors, the connection between a person's experiences and relationships, and the emergence of specific behaviors.

2. **Diminish resentment toward money**

Some people experience specific financial emotions that have an impact on both their financial and mental health decisions. Financial therapists can aid in easing anxiety, fear, guilt, and other negative emotions.

3. Seek wise financial counsel

Financial therapists can provide useful financial advice based on your needs and circumstances. This may enhance your capacity for making decisions.

4. Consider ways to make your situation better

You can develop more wholesome financial beliefs and behaviors through your therapy sessions. In addition, you will be better able to organize your finances.

Who Would Benefit from Financial Therapy?

While everyone can gain from financial therapy, some people require it. Unfortunately, these are people whose money problems hamper personal and interpersonal relationships.

Some people are unsure of the behaviors or methods best suited for their financial situation. Others might have trouble determining the most effective ways to manage, save, and spend money. This justifies the value of financial counseling. The information below will help you to know if you might profit from financial counseling:

- People with financial difficulties

Financial distress may manifest as compulsive spending, concealing purchases, or avoiding financial statements. To end an abusive relationship, whether it be abusive physically, emotionally, or financially, requires a lot of bravery on the part of the woman.

- Individuals overcoming addiction

Commitment and assistance are necessary for addiction recovery. A financial therapist can help with debt repayment, encourage savings plans, and develop the best strategy for achieving economic recovery.

- Women who are abused in relationships

To end an abusive relationship, whether it be abusive physically, emotionally, or financially, requires a lot of bravery on the part of the woman. To regain independence, sound financial planning is also necessary. A financial therapist can be useful in this situation.

- Individuals with specific disorders

People with obsessive-compulsive disorder (OCD) or post-traumatic stress disorder (PTSD) should consider financial therapy if their condition affects their ability to manage their finances.

Successful financial planning and management is the key to your success. Financial therapists are trained to help you sort through your finances and make informed decisions. In addition, they can respond to inquiries regarding taxes, insurance, investments, or other monetary-related issues.

The Takeaways

- Financial therapists provide counseling services that allow you to understand your personal goals and values, so they can help you achieve them in a way that makes sense.
- Always make financial preparations for the future.
- Financial problems may negatively impact your mental health.

2

YOUR WILLINGNESS TO PLAN AND SAVE

When planning to save for your retirement, it is important to be intentional about it. However, don't assume you have it all planned out without setting financial goals. Financial goals are a way to track your progress in reaching the life you want. They are a tool for you to use to help you achieve your long-term financial goals. The main purpose of establishing values is to help you plan for the future and ensure you're on track with your spending so that you can reach your goals. It's important to create some financial goals so that you can measure your progress toward achieving them. And it's also helpful to have an idea of what they are so that they're something tangible to work toward. Financial goals help you prevent financial problems and make it easier to achieve your dreams. For instance, if you want to purchase a new car but don't have enough money saved up, setting a financial goal can help you decide what kind of car you want and how much money you need to save up from now until then.

Your financial goals should be detailed and specific, so you can see exactly what you need to do to reach them. For example, you might want to pay off your credit card debt, save up for a vacation, or build up your emergency fund. Anyway, ensure you know what it is you're trying to accomplish! When writing out your financial goals, try not to get too caught up in what's trendy right now—you should always be thinking about what will make you happiest in the long run. When you're making financial goals, it's important to remember that your long-term financial goals don't have to be your only objective. You can have multiple short-term goals related to each other and then work on those as you move along toward reaching your longer-term goal. As you proceed reading, you will learn about establishing these plans and how fear and anxiety prevent you from achieving this planning.

5 STEPS TO SETTING YOUR FINANCIAL GOALS IN 2022

When setting financial goals, some important steps are helpful. Below are steps that may help you make the right decision concerning your finances and improve your ability to reach your financial goals:

Give your money a "job"

Giving your money a job means taking an interest in where your money goes and then putting it to work for you by investing it in something that will improve your life—something that could grow and multiply over time. This can include anything from buying stocks to saving for retirement or even starting a business. It's about ensuring that no matter how much money you earn, there's always an opportunity for more.

Giving your money a job is about ensuring you have money in the bank before you need it. It's about being aware of how much money you have, what is coming in, and what is going out. It's about keeping track of your expenses and knowing where the money is going so you can budget for what comes next. It is about ensuring you are using your resources efficiently and effectively. It's not just about having an emergency fund—it's about making sure that everything else in your life is taken care of as well so that when something unexpected happens, everything will still be there for you to handle it. Giving your money a job is about being ready for the future—knowing what's coming up and making sure you're prepared for anything that might come up so that when it does show up, everything will be ready to go!

Giving your money a job is, quite literally, giving your money back to you. It's a way to ensure your money is doing work for you, rather than sitting idly in the bank or under your mattress. When you give your money a job (and we're not talking about the kind of job where it sits around waiting for you to tell it what to do), you're actually encouraging it to grow and multiply itself by reinvesting in itself. That means, instead of having a bunch of cash just sitting around waiting for something to happen—like paying for groceries or going on vacation—you can actually let that cash do something useful. So how do you give your money a job? Well, if you're using cash, all it takes is writing out a check at the end of each month so that it can go back into circulation and be used again without being withdrawn from circulation first. If you're using credit card debt instead of cash (which most people do), there are some great ways to give your debt-based financial system some breathing room as well.

Categorize each financial goal

The first step to categorizing your financial goals is figuring out where you stand right now. Your financial goals can either be short-term, mid-term, or long-term goals.

Short-term goals

Short-term goals are goals you want to achieve within a certain time frame, typically three months. You can have many short-term goals, and they may even overlap. For example, if you're just starting out, your short-term goals will probably be things like getting a credit card and paying down some debt. You'll also want to make sure you've saved enough money in case of an emergency. Other examples include saving money to buy a new computer, moving out of your parent's house, and getting a job.

Mid-term goals

Mid-term goals are goals you want to achieve in between short-term and long-term goals. They're not necessarily time-specific, but they still need to be achieved within the next three, six, or twelve months (depending on how far away the goal is from being completed). Examples include saving up for a vacation or paying off debt.

Long-term goals

Long-term goals are goals that take longer than six months—and sometimes much longer—to accomplish.

These are those lofty dreams that seem out of reach but aren't really impossible if we make a plan and put in the work. Of course, there's nothing wrong with dreaming big—if that's what inspires you most! But it's important to remember that these big projects take time and effort to complete, so divide them into simpler and smaller steps if necessary. Examples include setting aside money for retirement or starting a business.

Set a Target Date for Every Financial Goal

Setting a target date for each financial goal is the first step in creating a plan for your money. The target dates are important because they help you track where you're at regarding your goals, and they can help you ensure that if something goes wrong, it doesn't derail your plans. Of course, you can set a target date for when you want to achieve your financial goals, but that doesn't mean you have to stick with them forever.

Setting a target date for each financial goal is an important part of achieving your goals because it forces you to take action toward achieving those objectives. If you try to set up multiple targets at once, then it's more likely that they will be missed or forgotten about altogether. Instead, set one date per financial goal, make sure that date comes before any other dates on your list, take action on that day toward achieving your goal, create another date for achieving the next step in reaching your goal, etc. Perform these steps until you finally reach the final deadline, which marks the completion or fulfillment of one or more steps along the way. You will feel much more motivated about making progress toward reaching those goals than if there were no deadlines!

The first step is deciding what your financial goals are. This will help you establish what you want to achieve with your money so that when you set a target date for each goal, it will be easy to remember what you need to do next. When you know your financial goals, it's time to think about how long each goal should take. This helps establish how long it will take before you reach the next level of financial success. If a particular goal takes too long or requires too much work on your part, then perhaps that goal isn't right for where you're at right now—financially or mentally. Once you have decided on how long each goal should take and what it entails (and possibly even what type of organization or company will help), then it's time to set a target date for when each goal should be met!

Prioritize your financial objectives.

When starting a new financial plan, it can be tempting to simply jump right in and start saving money without thinking about which goal is most important. But there's a reason why we have to prioritize our goals when we first set up our financial plans: they're all equally important! When it comes to prioritizing your goals, you'll want to take into consideration three things:

- How urgent is this need? Is it something that is going to prevent me from being able to pay my bills in the near future?
- How likely am I to achieve this goal? How long will it take? What kind of effort does it require?

The first step to prioritizing your financial goals is to identify what they are. This will help you whether you have a lot of options or if there are only a few options that are truly important. Next, decide which financial goal is critical, which is need-based, and which is want-based. If a particular financial goal has to do with something that's important to you (like paying off student loans), it should be your top priority. But if it's just something that's nice to have (like having a new car), that can wait until later in the list. Once you are sure of your priorities, you can start thinking about how to get them done! There's no need for panic: even if it seems like things aren't going according to plan right now, don't let yourself become overwhelmed by it! Just take small steps toward achieving what matters most to you at this moment.

Know your net worth vs. what you still need to save.

To know how much you have vs. what you still need to save, you need to look at your net worth. Net worth is the difference between your liabilities and assets. Your assets are things you own, like savings accounts and stocks in your 401(k) plan or house, while your liabilities are things like car loans and credit card debt. You also want to know how much of your income goes toward saving for the future (or paying down debt). If you have not saved enough for your retirement or spending too much on other things (like clothing), then it's time for a financial check-up!

You can save more by knowing how much you have in your bank account versus what you still need to save. For example, if you have $1,250 and want to put $500 of it into your savings account and $500 into investing, that would leave you with $250 left over. That's the amount of money you can use for bills and other expenses each month.

You can use a few simple tools to know how much you have saved and what you still need to save. The first tool is a calculator that shows you the difference between your current balance and the amount you want to save. The next step is always to take a look at your paycheck stubs, which should be available online or at your workplace. After you have the numbers, it's time to calculate how much you need to put away every month in order to reach your goal by the end of the year—or sooner if possible! Of course, you'll want to make sure that this number is realistic and attainable.

Don't let fear and anxiety ruin your financial life.

Fear and anxiety are a waste of your time. They're also a waste of your money. Think about it: when you're afraid, you don't make good decisions. You can't make good decisions when you're anxious, either—you're too distracted by what-ifs and which "ifs" to focus on at the present moment. And that's bad news for your finances: if you don't know where you are going, how can you get there? So, the next time you feel the urge to drop everything and run away from something that's making you anxious, try this instead: take a deep breath, then focus on what's right in front of you—right now. Then, plan for what needs to happen next.

Note that there is a difference between worrying and being prepared. And if you're not careful with your money, it might ruin your financial life. I understand that you're afraid that something bad is going to happen to your money—and that you'll be left without any when it does. Here are the facts: first, the odds of something bad happening are pretty low. You will probably worry more about being hit by a bus than losing most of your savings to fraud or other problems. And even if you did lose all of it, there are plenty of ways to get back on track (like getting a loan). Secondly, if something bad does happen, chances are that you'll be able to deal with it in an effective way—just like most people who fall victim to fraud or theft do!

Below are Deepak Chopra's five tips for financial wellness that can help you overcome your fear and anxiety:

Don't spend money to impress people.

Many people have wasted their savings because of this. They buy stuff or do things with the aim of impressing people. That's such an unwise decision to make. To be financially healthy, don't spend what you have not earned to buy things that you do not need to impress people that you do not like. Funnily enough, the people you want to impress may not notice you. And if they do, what value would it add to your finances?

Put away 10% of your monthly income into a savings account.

Most times, people spend all their money on expenses and bills without remembering to save some. Most people have been trapped into not saving anything because they feel that what they earn is not enough. The bitter truth is that no one admits that they earn enough. And even if you don't earn enough, saving or not saving will not make it enough. Hence, it is advisable to save at least 10%

of your income. Make it like a rite that you should not miss for anything. When you are committed to your savings, it becomes easier to save more.

Look for a job that offers benefits.

When you want to get a job, try to seek jobs that offer you benefits like leave, health insurance, transportation, and wardrobe allowance, etc. Having such a job would help to reduce your expenses. Surely, you don't have to spend on some things when your job has already sorted them out. In other words, you will have more to save and less to spend.

Do not ignore your well-being, your body, mind, and emotions.

Many people are so carried away with their job and their source of income that they neglect their health and well-being. No matter how much you want to earn, neglecting your well-being is disastrous. If you don't take care of your physical and mental health, you are prone to illness. When you are unhealthy, you are more likely to spend much more than you would if you had paid attention to your health in the first place. In addition, taking care of your health doesn't have to cost you money. It can be as simple as getting enough sleep, eating well, exercising, and many more.

Make other people successful. Their success is also your success.

Most times, we get so carried away pursuing success that we don't care about the people around us. In all you do, try your best to make other people successful. When people get successful through you, you can count yourself as successful. There is this fulfillment you have when you know that you have helped people to accomplish their goals.

THE LINK BETWEEN MONEY AND MENTAL HEALTH

A lot of people are struggling with their financial or mental health because they have allowed one to affect the other. In fact, some don't know that money can affect their mental health. Learning how money is related to your mental health can help you if you are facing challenges or struggling.

Here are some ways your mental health can affect your finances:

– If you are feeling depressed, you may not be motivated to manage your money. It might make you feel like your financial life isn't worth investing effort into.

– Spending excessively can make you feel okay when depressed or feeling low. And as a result, you may overspend more than necessary.

– When struggling with your mental health, you might make some irrational financial decisions.

– You may earn lesser than usual if your mental health affects your work life or ability to study.

– Mental illness can make you avoid doing things relating to your finances, like opening bills or checking your account. In fact, it might make you stop thinking about anything related to money.

– You might pay more than usual if your mental illness affects your insurance.

As mental health can affect your finances, money problems also can affect your mental health. Here are some ways money can affect your mental health:

- Some situations, like calculating your bills or checking your credit account, might trigger panic, worry, or anxiety.
- When you overthink about money, you may end up having sleepless nights.
- If you don't have enough money, you may not afford what you need for your well-being. These things include water, heating, food, and therapy.
- Financial crises can also affect your relationship and social life. For example, lack of money can make you feel lonely or guilty about not affording the things you should have.

FEELINGS ASSOCIATED WITH MONEY

The thoughts of money can leave you with different kinds of emotions. Here are different feelings associated with money:

- When you spend money, you may feel guilty even when you can afford it. You may also feel guilty for seeking financial support—even in times when you need it the most.
- You might feel fearful about looking at your account details or contacting your bank.
- You might feel embarrassed for seeking financial support. Kindly know that we all have the right to have our needs met. Seeking financial help is a way that you maintain essential things like food and housing.
- Money might make you feel stressed. For instance, if you are pressured to fend for yourself and also support others. Trying to provide for your needs may leave you stressed if you don't know when to relax.
- If you are battling with financial crises for a long time, it might leave you worn out or tired.
- If you have had a negative experience with money, it may affect how you feel about money and even handle money.

MONEY AND YOUR MOOD PATTERN

It can help if you take time to reflect on your feelings about money. For instance, if you had little money while growing up or have struggled financially in the past, it might affect your mood in relation to money. To find out the reason for the changes in your mood, you could try to answer the following questions:

- Are there specific times that you mostly tend to spend money?
- Are there specific times that you mostly tend to save more?
- What's your mood after spending money?
- What's your mood after saving money?
- Do you have different feelings when you save and spend money?
- What are the feelings you have when you think about your finance?
- What part of dealing with money makes your mental health low? For instance, it could be things like opening envelopes, attending to your bills, appointments, being misunderstood, etc.

Keeping a journal of how and why you spend can help you feel better. You could also write down your feelings before and after spending.

Once you have a journal, you might better understand your money patterns and habits. Having a better understanding of how you feel about money could help you have proper plans ahead of tough times.

In conclusion, your willingness to plan and save for your retirement is important. You may not be able to achieve anything tangible concerning your finances if you don't have financial goals. Your financial goals will help you to stay focused and be determined to achieve them. When setting goals for your finances, it is important to set specific, realistic, and time-bound goals. One of the steps to setting your financial goals is knowing what you earn vs. what you need, which will help you make better financial decisions. Furthermore, fear and anxiety can be a hindrance to making decisions that will enhance your finances. So, don't allow them to stop you. In addition, you might have changes in mood when dealing with money; hence, you should know what those moods are and why you have them. Once you know, those things will help you better prepare for tough times that may affect your mood and mental health.

The Takeaways:

- The main purpose of financial goals is to help you plan for the future and make sure that you're on track with your spending so that you can reach your goals.
- You will be able to save more money by knowing how much you have in your bank account versus what you still need to save.
- When you are committed to your savings, it becomes easier to save more.
- Neglecting your well-being is disastrous, no matter how much you want to earn.

3

YOUR OPPORTUNITIES TO PLAN AND SAVE

There are many avenues and opportunities to cushion your life after retirement by saving and making the best financial decisions, which will be discussed and explained in this chapter. At the same time, we are discussing the different ways you can save and plan, including theories and exposing you to FPR literacy. This chapter will be taking things up a notch a little bit. This is the chapter you might want to pay a lot of attention to. Over the years, as an FPR expert and educator, the most frequent inquiries have always been about what savings plan I would use. What is the perfect retirement plan for me? What is the best plan for my career?

This chapter will answer most of the questions you probably had when you picked up this book. In this chapter, we will discuss various retirement savings plans, investment plans, traditional plans, individual retirement accounts, thrift savings plans, and contribution plans. All these saving and planning opportunities will be discussed or explained broadly, including the pros and cons. We will be considering plans and options that are concordant with the times. What is the best retirement savings plan to adopt in the twenty-first century, 2022—2030? Planning in advance and considering all the options and considerations is vital for a comfortable retirement.

DEFINED CONTRIBUTION PLANS

Defined contribution plans are a type of pension payment plan for retirement that involves making contributions regularly by the employer or employee. Individual accounts will be set up for each participant. The contribution is usually a fixed percentage of an annual or monthly salary deducted by the employer or employee.

Defined contribution plans are employer-sponsored, which means it is kept afloat by the employer as a benefit to their employees. Then they both contribute to the plans, although in most cases, only the employer or employee makes a contribution regularly. One perk of a defined contribution plan is that the funds in an individual's personal account are not taxable. It remains tax-free while the funds remain in the account. This is because it is deducted pre-tax or post-tax. A pre-tax deduction is even more beneficial because it reduces an individual's taxable income.

With defined contribution plans, the funds deposited into an employee's account may be invested in the stock market, and its returns are then added to the employee's account. The defined contribution plan is available in countries such as the United States, the United Kingdom, Singapore, and France.

The defined contribution plan is widely used in the United States. In a workplace retirement plan such as a defined contribution, you can choose how much you want deducted to be added automatically to your individual account. Then it is deducted from your paycheck. A defined contribution plan gives individuals more control over how their money is invested. You can decide how much you want to set aside for investments, how risky you want to be, and what kind of investments you want to put your funds into. You can also decide when to buy or sell shares.

The Pros and Cons of a Defined Contribution Plan

The defined contribution plan is a common retirement plan for pension funds in most private institutions in the United States. One of its profound perks is that the funds in a personal account are sheltered from taxation until it is obtainable. It is also very beneficial; it can be invested and generate added profits; there is no immediate or concurrent deduction of taxes.

Let's go through a list of pros and cons. Before taking a job that offers a defined contribution plan, you should consider this:

+ Pros

1. A defined contribution plan gives individuals more control over how their money is invested. You can decide how much you want to keep aside for your retirement, how much you want to set aside for investments, how risky you want to be, and what kind of investments you want to put your funds into. You can also decide when to buy or sell shares.
2. A defined contribution plan increases the probability of having more money for yourself during retirement.
3. The funds in your personal account are portable; you can take the money with you when you move on to work in another company.
4. Your funds are also protected from pre-retirement inflation.

– Cons

1. The defined contribution plan is the costliest type of pension fund plan.
2. It is administratively complex.

3. A fixed payout is not based on the results of investments; you get a fixed payout regardless of the results of any investment.

INDIVIDUAL RETIREMENT ACCOUNTS (IRA)

An individual retirement account is a tax-deferred investment account that allows an individual to save on a defined contribution plan basis, money that grows and compounds in the long term. You do not have to involve your employer before opening an individual retirement account, which is why it is called a personal account. You can open a separate retirement account and save as long as you have an earned income. Individual retirement accounts can be opened through a bank, investment company, personal broker, or online brokerage. You can also choose to run and hide.

An individual retirement account would be considered a defined contribution plan. You can decide to invest in various financial products such as stocks, bonds, mutual funds, or exchange-traded funds, including real estate. Financial products with high levels of risk are off-limits. The individual retirement account is strictly for retirement. Withdrawing your funds before the age of 59½ will attract a 10% penalty on your funds. However, there are some exceptions.

Many individual retirement accounts are available in the United States with different features, rules, pros, and cons.

They include Traditional IRAs, ROTH IRA, Spousal IRA, Rollover IRA, SEP IRA, and Simple IRA.

Let's take a look at each.

Traditional IRAs

The traditional IRA has no income limitations; it is an individual retirement account to which you can contribute funds pre-tax. Your money can grow tax-deferred, and income tax is paid on every withdrawal. The traditional IRA, formerly called regular IRA, was created in 1975 and is accessible by anyone without limitation of income. However, specific qualifications such as sufficient income, filing status, and availability of other retirement income may be made available. There is also a contribution limit; you can contribute an amount of $6,000 per annum, but if you are 50 or older, you can contribute $7,000.

The traditional IRA can be quite a beneficial retirement plan to consider. However, like all options, the pros and cons should be considered.

Why you should adopt a traditional IRA: the most common feature that makes the traditional IRA favorable is the rule allowing anyone with sufficient income to contribute to the account to open one.

+ Pros

1. There is no income limit to open or contribute to a traditional IRA.
2. Your contributions are tax-deferred.
3. You can pay for college or emergency expenses without paying an early withdrawal penalty; however, your withdrawal is taxable.
4. You can use up to $10,000 to pay for a first house without paying an early withdrawal penalty, but the withdrawal is taxable.

– Cons

1. Withdrawal before the age of 59½ attracts a penalty fee of 10% of the withdrawal.
2. You must begin withdrawal at the age of 72.

Roth Individual Retirement Account

The Roth IRA is a specific or unique kind of individual retirement account that allows an individual to save after-tax dollars that are tax-deferred even after withdrawal. Your contribution and earnings on the account can grow without being taxable and can be withdrawn after 59½; as long as the account has been open for five years or more, this is a primary benefit that mostly convinces the users of Roth IRA.

Your Roth IRA account can be funded by:

- Spousal contributions
- Conversions
- Rollover contributions
- Transfers
- Spousal IRA contributions

Roth IRA options for investments are pretty vast; cryptocurrencies, exchange-traded funds, mutual funds, stocks, bonds, money market funds, and certificates of deposits. However, while you cannot directly contribute cryptocurrency to your Roth account, there is a Bitcoin IRA.

The SIDRA—self-directed IRA is a particular type of Roth; in this type of pension fund plan, you get to manage your investment rather than the financial institutions. This makes it possible to have a broader range of options for investment opportunities, like real estate, gold, or franchise businesses. The maximum amount a person can contribute to a Roth account is $6,000; those 50 years or older can contribute $7,000.

With a Roth IRA account, you have to exercise a substantial level of consciousness. Firstly, you have to consider trading costs; you want to pick a provider with low service costs. A provider would recommend Interactive Brokers as they exchange zero dollars for every trade made, and they have zero fees. Look out for promotional discounts. If you already have an existing account with a bank or brokerage, look out for discounts they give to existing customers. Roth IRAs can also be insured.

The FDIC is set up to provide insurance protection up to $250,000 per depositor if your bank is FDIC-insured. However, if you have more than a single account, your accounts will be combined insured. For instance, suppose you have $150,000 in your Roth IRA and $250,000 in another account; your funds will be merged and insured. $150,000 and $250,000 add up to $400,000, but only $250,000 will be paid back to you.

Spousal IRAs

Spousal IRAs allow you to contribute to an IRA as a working spouse on behalf of your non-working spouse. It is simply a Roth or traditional IRA used by married couples. However, it is not a joint account, as it may be wrongly preconceived. A spousal IRA can be opened by an individual on behalf of a married partner and can be beneficial to you and your partner. Yet, this retirement option is mostly under discussion—however tremendously beneficial it may be. Only legally married couples who file joint taxes can be eligible for a spousal IRA.

With a spousal IRA, you can remain relaxed if your spouse gets laid off or has to stay home to take care of a family member, take some time off, or go back to school. Just know that your partner will get a comfortable retirement;

however, the contributing individual needs to be earning enough to contribute to their personal account and that of their spouse. A spousal IRA can take the form of a Roth IRA or a traditional IRA. The only difference is that it is set up in the name of an individual's partner and belongs to the person whose name it is opened under. A spousal IRA also gives you and your married partner a tax advantage, which depends on the income level of the contributing partner.

You can both elect to do a traditional IRA. This can be a wise option because it allows taxable income to be reduced. You can also choose to save in a Roth IRA, in which you and your spouse can contribute post-tax income and then be able to withdraw your money free from taxes in the future. As a contributing or earning spouse, having a retirement plan at work could reduce the amount of money you can contribute to your spousal IRA. You can put more money into a traditional IRA instead of a spousal IRA, but you do not get the tax benefits with a traditional IRA as you might get with a spousal IRA.

Saving in a spousal IRA can benefit every family, especially when your partner does not earn enough or is not earning a living. In addition, spousal IRAs will always be handy in cushioning the adverse effects of retirement. In the case of a divorce, spousal IRAs can also be helpful. As the dependent spouse, you still have your future secure and do not have to start from scratch.

Rollover IRA

A rollover IRA is the best way to handle an old 401(k). Of course, other options exist, such as leaving it in your old company and cashing out. Cashing out could be the worst option unless you deposit it into an account for savings. On the other hand, a rollover IRA allows you to transfer the funds in your old 401(k) to another in a new company should you be fired. When done correctly, the money in your IRA is tax-deferred and does not trigger taxes or penalties for early withdrawal.

Let's go through a list of essential things you need to know before attempting to move the funds from your 401(k) into an IRA:

1. You can choose a Roth IRA or a traditional rollover IRA. Traditional IRAs do not come with withdrawal taxes until withdrawal, while a Roth rollover account comes with withdrawal taxes. However, funds become tax-free after the age of 591/2. If you want to minimize your retirement tax bill, a Roth IRA might be a better option.
2. Next, you will need to choose your rollover IRA provider. You could use an online broker to take personal control over your savings and investments. A suitable online broker should have excellent customer service, low account charges, and a wide selection of low-cost investments. You could also

decide to choose Robo advisors, which will be half less costly than a human advisor and would help you angle your portfolio efficiently.
3. There is a 60-day rule for an indirect rollover to get your money into an IRA; failure to do that will attract an early withdrawal penalty of 10% of your money.
4. Twenty percent is withheld by your company to pay taxes on your distribution; you will need to pay additional taxes.
5. You can continue to contribute to a rollover IRA.

Rollover IRAs are the best solution for individuals looking to leave their present workplace for another and who are worried about their 401(k) funds.

SEP IRA

If you are a small business owner or self-employed, then the simplified employee pension IRA is probably the best option. It is a form of individual retirement account that an employer or self-employed person can establish. SEP IRAs work with higher annual contribution limits than other standard IRAs. In addition, SEP IRAs can be rolled over and enjoy the same tax benefits as traditional IRAs. However, the contributions are tax deductible and are not tax-deferred.

SEP IRAs are best for business owners with few employees or no employees. The business owner can contribute to retirement plans at discretionary eligibility. If an employee has worked with you as a business owner for three years, you need to contribute to them. Employees can also own and control their accounts. A business owner also needs to make equal contributions for employees; this is why it is probably best for business owners with few employees. One perk of a SEP IRA is that you do not have to make contributions per annum; it is also very flexible and easy to set up and register.

Simple IRA

The simple IRA is a retirement plan for small businesses with fewer employees than 100. It is similar to other standard IRAs but is easier to set up. It has the same distribution, rollover, and investment types but a lower contribution limit. The contributions in a simple IRA are also taxed and enable employees to have a better retirement. It is less costly to start up a simple IRA and operate it; it is also beneficial for employees because they can contribute to the IRAs and exercise considerable freedom over it. You can choose other stocks and bonds if you do not want to engage in the mutual funds selected by your employer. Simple IRAs have some cons, such as the penalty for early withdrawals and loan limitations.

Traditional IRA	R o t h IRA	Spousal IRA	Rollover IRA	SEP IRA	Simple IRA
Grows tax-deferred	Can pay taxes before contrib ution.	Can either be a traditional or Roth IRA.	Can either be a Roth or traditional IRA.	Grows tax-deferred	For small business owners.
Can save in a traditional IRA while saving in a 401(k) plan.	Can withdr aw contrib utions at any time.	Earning individual can still save in other plans for themselves.	Can still be managed by individuals.	Very flexible and easy to manage.	Easy and flexible to set up.
No income limit.	Income limit.	Cannot be held jointly. Earning partners earn enough to cover an IRA too. Belongs solely to the dependent partner.	Income limit.	No income limit as long as you have a business.	No income limit.
$6,000 contribution limit per annum.	$6,000 contrib ution per annum.	Can contribute up to $12,000 a year.	Taxes are withheld.	No Roth options.	Employees can contribute, with a limit.
Can withdraw money at age 591/2 penalty-free or earlier.	You can withdr aw money at age 591/2 penalty -free or earlier.	Withdrawal before 591/2 attracts penalties.	A 10% penalty occurs for not shaving your withdrawal back after 60 days due to the 60-day rule.	Withdrawal before the age of 591/2 Is treated as a taxable income.	Pay income tax on any withdrawal unless you are of the age of 591/2.

The Solo 401(k) Plan

The solo 401(k) plan is for business owners without employees. It can also be used to cover your spouse. The rules do not allow full-time employees; it is a solo retirement plan, and you know what solo means. It has no restrictions on age or income.

The limit for a solo 401(k) contribution is $61,000. Let's talk about the perks of a solo 401(k). You can get significant tax advantages with a traditional 401(k), contributions reduce your taxable income, and your distributions will be taxed as ordinary income in retirement. A Roth 401(k) comes with no initial tax break, and your distributions in retirement are tax-free. The Roth 401(k) would be suitable if your income is going to be higher in retirement.

Solo 401(k) plans can be opened at most online brokers. To open one, you will need an employer identification number, you will need to provide a plan adoption agreement, and you will also need to complete an account application. Once you have done that, you will have access to the investment options offered by the broker, including mutual funds, exchange-traded funds, index funds, and individual stocks and bonds. You can also use Robo advisors to help manage the funds in your solo 401(k) account. Robo advisors are AIs programmed to provide automated financial guidance and services. The guidance provided is subjected to an algorithm and is generated by the firsthand gathering of information on a user or client through an online survey and then automatically investing for a user or a client based on preexisting data. So, if you do not want to think about your money and investments, your Robo advisor can do that for you.

+ Pros

1. You have unlimited investment options with a solo 401(k) account.
2. You will have higher contribution limits.
3. There is an allowance for a hardship withdrawal choice.
4. There is a participant loan option.
5. You can borrow for business funding or investment.

– Cons

1. You need zero employees to be eligible for a solo 401(k).
2. The IRS requires you to file an annual report on Form 5500-SF if the account has $250,000 or more assets at the end of the year. If your assets are less than $250,000 at the end of the year, you may be exempted.
3. For the account to be active, your contributions have to be regular.

Traditional Pensions

Traditional pensions are defined benefit retirement plans; the benefit plan provides monthly lifetime retirement benefits. The benefit plan functions best in a system that rewards long-term service; the longer you work, the higher your benefits will be. If you plan to stay at a firm or company for a long time, then the plan will be best for you. However, traditional pensions have become less used in the private sector. It is a system that can still be considered, however. The traditional pension requires and obliges an employer to make regular contributions to a fund set up to pay employees after retirement. However, it is costly to private employers. Hence, several retirement plans have replaced it. It is still mainly used in public service, and about 15% of the private sector still uses the traditional pension plan.

There are two types of traditional pensions:

1. Defined benefit plan.
2. Defined contribution plan.

With a defined benefit plan, the employer contributes to a pool of money to pay employees in retirement. However, the defined contribution plan requires that the employer regularly contributes to individual accounts of the employees. With defined benefit plans, the employee receives a regular and specific payment in retirement, unlike defined contribution plans that allow for investments and can yield profits.

Withdrawals from defined benefit plans are taxable upon withdrawal.

+ Pros

1. It is less risky for the employees.
2. There is a guaranteed retirement income for life.
3. It encourages employee retention.
4. There is an adjustment for inflation.
5. Employees do not usually need to make contributions.
6. You can pass it on to a beneficiary or next of kin. The pension will pay your beneficiary a percentage if you die before 75%.

− Cons

1. As an employee, you do not have control over investments.
2. It is less flexible when it comes to withdrawals.
3. If an employer experiences financial difficulties, then you may receive less.
4. Your savings are only available for you when you are 60 or 65.

Guaranteed Income Annuities (GIAs)

GIAs are contracts. How does a GIA work? If you have cash or funds you are unwilling to invest due to volatile stock options; then you can sign a GIA before turning your money over for a guaranteed payout in retirement from a desired fixed age. Trying to get an early payout may be difficult. After all, it is a contract. You might want to hold out some cash and not put all your money in a GIA. Some GIAs might have high fees as well. A GIA is a type of life insurance contract and can be an excellent cushion for bankruptcy; it can also provide you with a stream of income for your life after retirement.

+ Pros

1. Taxes are deferred until withdrawal.
2. It is a means to get a steady stream of income.

− Cons

1. GIAs are complex and rigid; that is, they are not a flexible guarantee.
2. The fees are much more expensive than an IRA or a 401(k).
3. Withdrawals are taxed as ordinary income, which translates into higher tax rates.
4. A GIA lacks liquidity.

Federal Thrift Savings Plan

The federal savings plan is a retirement and investment plan for federal employees in the United States, including workers in uniformed services. It is like a defined contribution plan in the private sector, except that it is open to federal workers. The benefits of a thrift savings plan (TSP) include automatic payroll contributions and matching contributions from the agency where you are employed. In addition, there are options for a traditional TSP that is not taxable until withdrawal or a Roth TSP, which allows for vast investment options and after-tax contributions so that an employee doesn't have to pay tax after withdrawal in retirement. The contribution limit for a TSP in the United States is $20,500.

With a TSP, you can invest in the following options: The Government Securities Investment (G) Fund, The Fixed-Income Index Investment Fund (F), The Common-Stock Index Investment (C) Fund, The Small-Capitalization Stock Index Investment (S) Fund, The International-Stock Index Investment (I) Fund and Specific Life-Cycle (L) Funds. You can have an IRA and a TSP simultaneously, and even if you do not contribute to your TSP, the government will still contribute 1% of your annual salary. The TSP is quite beneficial because of its low investment fees. Having an IRA and a TSP is also a smart move because that way, you can contribute money each year.

Cash Balance Plans

This plan comes with an option of a lifetime annuity. The employer will credit the employee's credits with the option of a lifetime annuity. With a cash balance plan, the employer credits an employee's account with a percentage of their yearly compensation plus interest charges. Changes in the portfolio cannot affect the retirement benefits to be paid out; the company bears all losses and does not affect the yearly contributions. It is maintained on an individual basis rather than a pool of money. With a cash balance plan, you receive a stated amount of money for a lifetime.

Cash Value Life Insurance Plan

This retirement plan provides coverage for the policy holder's life. It occurs at a cash value that can be accessed even after death. Therefore, it is a wise option if you are looking to provide financial security for a beneficiary. Cash value allows you to build value over time in an insurance policy. It is flexible because its cash value can be taken out as a loan or withdrawal or used to pay the policy premium. However, the cash value doesn't begin to accrue until two to five years after it has passed.

Non-Qualified Deferred Compensation Plans

This type of compensation has been earned by an employee but not yet received from an employer because it has not been transferred to an employee. Therefore, it cannot be counted as taxable income. It is also known as a 409 plan. Savings are tax-deferred in the non-qualified deferred compensation plan (NQDC) until employees reach retirement. It does not have a limit on expenses. It can be used for expenses, such as education and travel. However, the NQDC is not protected in bankruptcy; you lose your savings if your company goes bankrupt or through financial difficulties. If you earn highly and have exhausted all other savings options, NQDC is a great option. It is referred to as an excess benefit plan.

The Takeaways

You need to choose the right and compatible plans that will benefit you and your spouse when it comes to financial ease. Saving in America can be challenging, coupled with taxes and saving for your child's college, paying rent, mortgages, daily expenses, and money spent on taking care of aged relatives. However, using the prime information in this chapter will save you a lot on expenses. Analyze and decide what retirement option is best for you. Never forget how saving and planning for retirement are beneficial and vital. You will need all the financial help you can get when you are aged and living in retirement.

Ready to make a smart choice?

4

FINANCIAL PLANNING FOR RETIREMENT

The American Dream is a life of financial security, but for many, it is a dream. For many seniors, the dream is to retire with the resources needed to live comfortably. To do that, you need to plan for your retirement and know how much money you can expect in retirement. With the right financial tools and planning, you can achieve your financial security goals during retirement. This chapter will help you make sure that happens by helping you plan for the future.

The first step toward retirement planning is to look at what you have monetarily and what you will need to live on in retirement. Then, consider what kind of lifestyle you want in retirement and start saving money for it now. If necessary, work with an advisor so they can help you determine how much money is needed to fund your retirement goals.

Once that's done, it's time to figure out how much debt you have and how much income will be available each month when you are retired. Next, decide if any assets could help pay those debts or fund your retirement income needs once they're gone (like home equity). Finally, decide if any other requirements may need to be addressed (like health care costs), and then keep track of all this information as it changes over time so that it doesn't get forgotten or overlooked.

DEMOGRAPHICS FACTOR

Demographics play an important role in retirement planning. Demographics refer to the characteristics of a person's age, sex, race, and religion. These demographic factors are covered in information from the Unites States Census Bureau (USCB), including how many seniors there are in the country and how old they are when they die. The demographics of all the factors going into retirement planning, like gender and age, are changing. This presents financial planners with a new set of challenges when determining people's needs for retirement. There are many ways to examine demographics and the different factors influencing them. Still, when analyzing for retirement planning purposes, you can use two primary demographics: age and gender. Millions of baby boomers in the workforce know the challenge of retiring and starting over. In addition, the US is one of the most populous countries in the world, and it continues to grow. That makes planning for your future with a retirement advisor prudent and even more difficult than ever.

The world's aging population is a critical issue for countries worldwide. The number of people aged 65 years and over is expected to double by 2050, and this demographic shift will impact many aspects of society. The challenge for governments, businesses, and individuals is to plan for this change to ensure they can respond effectively.

Aging and Health: 'A global perspective by the World Health Organization (WHO) highlights some key challenges governments face as they plan for their future healthcare systems. These include:

Population aging: an increase in the number of older people (65 years plus).

Health concerns: rising disease burdens, increased risk factors, and reduced healthcare resources.

Cultural differences: different expectations about healthcare among diverse groups living within a country.

To reiterate, the challenge is that the population is aging. The number of people who are above 65 years of age will increase by almost one-third over the next two decades. As a result, many older people will require financial planning for their retirement years.

This is because many retirees are not receiving adequate pensions or other income from the state or work. In addition, many families struggle with high levels of debt to support their members during their retirement years. Because these factors are so prevalent across different countries around the world, many experts believe that governments urgently need to provide more financial support for older people facing poverty during retirement.

The challenge of population aging is a significant one for many countries. This is because many countries are facing an increasing number of people living longer, with a decline in the number of working-age people available to support a growing number of older people.

The challenge to financial planners is not just that the population is aging but that this may have a significant impact on financial planning. The extent to which this will affect financial planning depends on how much governments support or facilitate retirement planning and how much private sector providers prepare for such a change in their business models and services.

In addition to supporting retirement planning, governments also have other important issues concerning population aging. For example:

- How do we encourage people to plan for old age?
- How do we encourage healthy lifestyles?

- How can we help those who need assistance but cannot access it?

The aging population is one of the biggest challenges facing the world. In Australia, for example, the population of older Australians has been growing faster than the overall population, causing an age-related proportion of the population to rise quickly.

The demographic characteristics of this group are changing and evolving. For example, they have lower participation rates in the workforce than younger Australians, but many are seeking to stay active in their retirement years and pursue new interests and activities.

Older people are also living longer. Expectancy at birth rose by more than five years between 1983 and 2009 and is expected to continue growing due to improvements in health and longevity over time. This fact alone represents a significant challenge for governments, employers, families, and individuals alike, who must plan to ensure that they can provide adequate support for aging populations.

ECONOMIC SECURITY FOR SENIORS

Economic security for seniors is an essential priority for the Government of Canada. The Government is committed to helping Canadians meet their retirement income needs and protect their savings through a range of programs and tax measures designed to provide greater financial security for Canadian families.

Economic Security for Seniors provides information on how the Government of Canada has promoted economic security in retirement since 2005. The Financial Security in Retirement Act (FSA) was enacted in 2005 to support seniors and other Canadians who could lose their houses as a result of unforeseen circumstances like illness or unemployment. Under this legislation, Canadians who have exhausted their Registered Retirement Savings Plans (RRSPs) can access $2,000 annually from their Registered Retirement Income Fund (RRIF) account for up to five years following an unexpected event. The FSA also includes a hardship exemption which allows qualifying Canadians with low incomes to withdraw all or part of their RRSP funds without penalty if they face economic hardship due to an unforeseen event.

The economic security of seniors is a significant concern for both governments and businesses. They need to be able to live comfortably and independently, but they also need to have the means to make ends meet in old age. This section looks at some of the critical issues seniors face regarding their economic security.

The first issue is the value of their home. For many, their house has been the primary source of wealth accumulation over the years. They may have built up equity that can be drawn down as they need it, or perhaps that can be passed on to their children. But if they want to pass on assets such as shares or property, then they will need to consider how they would like them transferred into registered retirement savings plans (RRSPs). This can be done by having an estate plan. However, if it is not adequately prepared at death, then it may not work out as expected when the time comes to make transfers from RRSPs into other accounts or sell off assets in the end.

Economic security for seniors is a crucial goal for the Government of Ontario. The province's plan to provide new seniors with more support and financial security is already underway. They have also developed programs, policies, and services to help our older adults remain in their homes and communities as long as possible. Additionally, we are working to make sure that all senior citizens can find reasonable housing and fulfill their fundamental needs. We are investing $50 billion in healthcare, home care, and education as part of this plan, social assistance, and other support for Ontario's older adults over the next ten years. Retirement planning is a lifelong process that starts with creating a plan. Retirement planning aims to create a financial plan that will provide security when you retire. It's important to note that retirement planning isn't just about saving money; it's also about earning enough income to live comfortably in retirement.

This section provides general guidelines on how much you should save for retirement. Still, different types of retirement plans and strategies can help you further diversify your investments and grow them over time.

THE ROLE OF THE NATIONAL COUNCIL ON AGING (NCOA)

The goal of the National Council on Aging (NCOA) is to support older individuals in living effectively in their own homes, maintaining their independence and health, and making decisions that are best for them. To achieve these goals, NCOA provides programs and services that promote health and wellness, assist people with disabilities, provide financial planning, and help seniors access social services.

Health & Nutrition

The NCOA offers a comprehensive nutrition education program to schools, hospitals, community centers, and senior centers across the state. The program addresses the four fundamental nutrition principles:

1. Keep your blood sugar stable.
2. Eat enough food.
3. Eat plenty of fruits and vegetables.
4. Avoid too much fat.

Debts and Savings

The NCOA helps clients manage their debt with education on how credit card debt can affect one's credit rating. They also offer a free "Debt Management Workshop" for those who have outstanding debts or want to improve their finances by reducing their debt load. A critical aspect of retirement planning is understanding how to protect your assets from inflation and taxes. You may have a retirement plan through an employer or a program offered by your employer's retirement plan provider. You can use your employer's 401(k) plan, for instance, to make contributions if it exists but remember that if you leave your job and change employers, you will lose the opportunity to contribute to this plan.

These are issues that a skilled financial advisor can assist you with. A financial planner will review your assets, debts, and income so that they can recommend the most tax-efficient way to reduce debt and maximize returns on investment. A financial planner will also work with you in developing a long-term investment strategy that meets your goals while minimizing risk. Finally, they will help you identify potential pitfalls in the market and provide suggestions for managing those risks. When you retire, your financial security is essential. In addition, you want to know that you can maintain your lifestyle in the years ahead.

AGING AND FINANCIAL INCLUSION

Many industrialized and emerging nations are seeing a sharp increase in the number of older adults and their share of the population; still, other countries will see a similar increase in the years to come. In 2050, the UN projects that there will be nearly two billion individuals globally who are 60 or older, with one in five people living in developing nations (UN, 2017).

First of all, aging populations will generate various opportunities, albeit variations between nations may exist. As working lives lengthen and formality rises, older employees in all economies will drive demand for new or extra financial goods and services. They engage in the so-called "Longevity Economy," which greatly impacts economic growth potential. Additionally, the impact won't be restricted to high-income nations. Older employees will continue to spend money as populations age in less developed countries. With the proper infrastructure and legislative frameworks, younger adults can use formal savings products to plan for their expected longevity. As a share of total assets, assets held and managed by or on behalf of older consumers will grow in importance. If used wisely, it can support productive activities, including small businesses.

Longer life also makes new life trajectories possible. These may include various training and employment opportunities, entrepreneurial pursuits, more time spent with families and communities, and opportunities to engage in leisure or philanthropic endeavors in the upcoming longer lifespan, depending on individual circumstances and economic prosperity.

Because they have less money saved, less income, and more costs as they age, people are more prone to encounter financial difficulty and poverty. Adults may be less likely to know about or have access to financial resources that can help them at different times of their lives. They plan for a long life in less developed economies with weak economic infrastructure. In nations with access to such services, costs for long-term care, adapted housing, physical help, and medical and dental care are likely to consume a larger share of household budgets. While health problems are more prevalent in older persons, their onset and severity can differ. Additionally, older individuals are different in terms of income, savings, housing, education, employment, and families, as well as traits like gender or location. Therefore, financial inclusion initiatives should be tailored to the requirements and circumstances of each individual.

STRENGTHEN DIGITAL AND FINANCIAL LITERACY

Financial literacy is critical for giving people the skills and confidence to manage their finances. To this end, working with governments, banks, regulators, and other stakeholders on several initiatives to:

- Increase the availability of financial services in low-income countries.
- Improve education about financial products and services.

- Raising awareness of the dangers associated with high-risk investments (such as equities).
- Initiate research and development in low-income countries to improve products and services that provide better access to financial products.

In a world of increased technology, we must be able to use it to our advantage. However, we must also understand how technology works and how it can be used to our benefit. The WHO's response to this issue is to promote the use of digital technologies for financial literacy and education, as well as to increase public awareness about financial topics in general.

Economic security for seniors is a significant challenge in the US today, as more older Americans are living longer and healthier lives. The solution lies in improving the lives of older Americans through economic security, including preserving the social safety net, reducing income inequality, and taking steps to make communities more livable for seniors. Among the various ways that experts can assist seniors with their financial planning are the following:

- Assist seniors in understanding their retirement needs and options.
- Help seniors make informed decisions about saving and spending.
- Guide seniors in making intelligent investments.

- Offer guidance regarding estate planning issues, including assets and beneficiaries.

Innovative financial services via the internet using algorithms may be possible to spot behaviors or acts that suggest a customer may have erred or misunderstood something. This could be very helpful for older persons who are less at ease utilizing digital financial services. Such technology can also be used to spot potentially fraudulent transactions and stop them from going through, for instance, by using artificial intelligence to spot and ban voice phishing phone calls or potentially dangerous emails. However, even though simple digital technologies can deliver crucial information and make decision-making more accessible, many elderly individuals prefer paper-based interactions.

THE WHO RESPONSE

The World Health Organization response aims to help people take charge of their financial futures by strengthening their ability to make informed decisions and by allowing them to navigate the complex world of retirement planning. The WHO response to the financial inclusion of older people is being developed in line with the work of the Financial Inclusion Task Force (FITF). The G20 leaders established the FITF in 2014 to address the challenges faced by low- and middle-income countries (LMICS) in closing the gap between rich nations and LMICS on financial inclusion. The

FITF has published a series of reports which outline vital recommendations for addressing financial inclusion challenges in LMICS.

In 2016, the WHO launched a Financial Inclusion Global Strategy (GSI), which aims to "address gaps in access to financial services" that affect older adults and other vulnerable groups worldwide. Through this strategy, the WHO is working with partners to ensure that all older adults have access to quality health services, including direct support for healthcare providers who provide these services.

The WHO response is focused on three key areas:

1. Income and employment.
2. Support lifetime financial planning.
3. Strengthen digital and financial literacy.

Women should make plans because, as we have stated before, they often have fewer retirement savings than men do. Here are some tips:

Consider a 401(k) or HSA.

Women should consider setting up a 401(k) or a Health Savings Plan (HSA) if they don't already have one. The money in these accounts is tax-deferred, which means you'll pay taxes on earnings later when you're in a lower tax bracket. That's especially important for women because they earn less than men and have lower incomes until they retire.

Look at the employer match.

If you make enough annual contributions, many employers will match your donations. For every $1 you provide, the company will give an extra dollar. A company may match up to 3 percent of base pay or 3 percent of base salary, whichever is higher. If your employer offers a match but doesn't meet your eligibility requirements, ask about setting up an IRA (an individual retirement account). Think about funds outside your employer's plan—especially if no match is available.

GENDER DIFFERENCES WHEN PLANNING FOR RETIREMENT

Retirement planning is a big deal. But it can be overwhelming. If you're a woman, you might wonder what to do with your savings. Should you put it in an IRA or a 401(k)? Or maybe you should use it for some of your down payment on a house. Or maybe you're interested in saving for your children's education or buying that dream vacation home. Maybe you'd want to spend more time with your loved ones and friends.

It's all fair game regarding retirement planning—but there are some critical differences between how men and women approach the topic. For example, a woman is more likely to have a lower salary than her male partner, which will impact retirement savings. Additionally, women are more likely to hold low-paying employment, which means they'll have less money to put into their 401(k)accounts.

The average woman who has maxed out her 401(k) contributions will have a nest egg of $236,000 at retirement. Likewise, the average man who has maxed out his 401(k) gifts will have a nest egg of $275,000 at retirement. For women, retirement savings could be even smaller if they don't take advantage of employer matching contributions (often 50% or more).

Women frequently delay financial preparation for retirement until they're forced to decide how much to save. Therefore, women don't become the breadwinners in their households because they are left with less disposable income than their partners.

Women are also less inclined to have access to employer-sponsored retirement plans like 401(k)s or 403(b)s "as already mentioned" and tend to make less money than men. When it comes to retirement savings, these differences can result in significant gaps between what women and men are able and willing to save each month. Women who want to retire early might not be able to afford traditional retirement plans, so they must consider other options.

Women who want to retire early should consider a 401(k) or HSA plan. The difference between these two accounts is that the 401(k) requires you to save money at work and then contribute money out of your paycheck before taxes are taken out, while the HSA allows you to put away pre-tax money and withdraw it tax-free when you're older.

How the Gender Income Gap Impacts Women's Retirement

The gender income gap is a massive problem for women, impacting their ability to retire comfortably. It acts as a major reason a high number of women delay retirement or work past their ideal retirement age.

The gender income gap exists because men earn more money than women. That means that women have less discretionary income than men. This can be problematic for retirees because they often need more money for healthcare or travel expenses. So if you're a woman, it's even more critical to plan your retirement savings if you have dependents who rely on your income.

Before women can retire, they still have a long way to go. The gender income gap is more comprehensive than in any other country, and women's savings are much lower than men's. Women are more unlikely to be the family's primary breadwinner, so they have less money saved up for retirement than men. If there's any doubt about how much you'll need, consider this: for every $1 a man saves for retirement, his wife saves $0.83. That means that if your husband only saves $10,000 per year and you save $3,000 per year, he'll have $60,000 when he retires while you'll have only $40,000 —even though it's still possible for both of you to live off of your pensions and Social Security payments alone.

The excellent thing is that couples can save money in various ways together for retirement—including 401(k)s and HSAs (health savings accounts). You are not required to pick between the two; you are free to open both accounts simultaneously.

If we may digress for a moment, it should be mentioned that not all insurance plans are eligible for Health Savings Accounts. Your health insurance plan must be a so-called high deductible insurance plan (HDHP) for you to qualify for an HSA. So, not everyone can—or should—try to enroll in an HSA. It so happens that employers who offer high-deductible health plans may also offer HSAs. If yours does not, you can open a separate HSA if you have a qualifying HDHP.

The gender income gap is a big problem for women. It's also a big problem for men but for different reasons.

Due to this gap, as we have mentioned before, women tend to earn less than men and have lower retirement savings than men. Consequently, Social Security is typically the only source of retirement income for most women. Women also have fewer assets (such as stocks or bonds) than men and therefore have less cash flow available during retirement. So what can you do? First, consider starting an IRA if you are not eligible to participate in an employer-sponsored plan.

If possible, take advantage of your employer-sponsored pension plan if you're eligible for one (either through your employer or through self-employed status). If you cannot participate in an employer-sponsored plan, consider opening an IRA for up to $5,500 annually ($6,500 if you are 50 or older).

Maximize your 401(k) contributions by contributing at least $18,000 per year before tax into your 401(k) until age 70½ (or age 50 if disabled). An additional $1 in the form of an automatic paycheck deduction may be added if you're under age 50 or disabled.

UTILIZE SELF-EMPLOYMENT TO CLOSE THE RETIREMENT INCOME GAP

Self-employment is an alternative to traditional employment for closing the gender pay gap in retirement, depending on risk tolerance and financial means. A woman's wage ceiling is removed when she works for herself and is given control over any employer-sponsored retirement plans. In addition, numerous financial obstacles can be eliminated through self-employment, such as a lack of education and strict work hours that conflict with caregiving responsibilities.

The Takeaways

- Eighty percent of the world's elderly population will reside in low- and middle-income nations by 2050.
- The population is aging considerably slower than in the past.

- All nations must overcome significant obstacles to ensure their social and health systems are ready to benefit from this demographic transformation.
- Women have to stretch their retirement resources over more extended periods since they live longer than males, and they are more likely to become widowed.
- When making retirement plans, there are numerous considerations to keep in mind, and they can differ depending on several criteria, including gender.

5

STOP PROCRASTINATING ON YOUR RETIREMENT PLAN! HERE'S HOW!

If you want to pay off your debts, save money and retire early, there's no better time than now. Personal finance is a major concern for many people, even those who have retired and are comfortable with their financial lives. Procrastination may be an issue, as many find it difficult to plan for the future. Still, regardless of where you're at in life and your current financial situation, there are ways to approach this important aspect of retirement planning.

This chapter reminds me that my professional life has given me some insight into the characteristics of the human psyche and the variables that affect how people behave. It would be an understatement to say that it has been fascinating. Here are some important lessons I've learned based on my observations. These ideas are straightforward common sense derived from real life and real people.

What role do social, interpersonal, and affective factors play in planning? This study aims to investigate the psychosocial aspects of retirement financial planning. Financial planning is an interdisciplinary topic in which individuals and their families need knowledge of personal finances and finance professionals. At the same time, social scientists need to develop models that help understand how planners make important decisions about saving for retirement. This chapter will show you how to ensure your retirement plan is on track and help you know what you should be doing today to get there.

You can make a plan to meet your basic goals after you are aware of your retirement age, the kind of lifestyle you choose, and the amount of income you'll require. You won't have enough time to close the potential gap between spending and retirement income if you wait until the last minute. Another common misunderstanding is the idea that your company or the human resources department at work would provide you with all the knowledge you need to build your financial plans for retirement. As a result, most people wait for their employer to start the retirement planning process. Sadly, the law does not force your employer to give you a pension or information on pensions. Thankfully, many firms offer pension plans to their staff members. These plans must provide you with the very minimum of details, like the date you will be eligible for a pension, the amount you will receive if you retire on various dates, and the methods for taking money out of your account. However, your employer is not required to inform you about other crucial retirement issues, including retirement planning, eligibility for National Insurance benefits, or the need for life and medical insurance in retirement.

WHY DO WE PROCRASTINATE?

Procrastination is a normal part of life. It allows us to experience the pleasure of doing something that feels good without facing the real consequences. This can be useful in everyday life as we move from one task to the next, but it also applies to achieving long-term goals. For example, we may delay starting a project because we are not sure how long it will take or how much effort it will require. We might also put off saving for retirement because we don't know how long it will take or what it might cost in terms of money and time.

However, there are times when procrastination can have negative consequences for our finances and personal relationships. For example:

- We might put off paying bills or meeting financial obligations because we don't want to face up to these payments.
- We may delay planning for retirement because we are afraid of facing up to the reality of having less disposable income later on in life.

- We may avoid asking a partner for help with household chores because we don't want them upset with us (it is easier just not to ask).

Reverse Priorities

Accept the "good" debt and stay away from the "bad" debt during these incredibly cheap interest rate periods. Like cholesterol, debt has both beneficial and negative aspects. In your 20s, 30s, and 40s, embrace 30-year mortgages; in your 50s and 60s, think about an eight, twelve, or fifteen-year mortgage. I've seen people proudly debt-free in their early 50s but are too frequently behind on their retirement funds. Your house won't be able to provide you with any retirement income, and starting your retirement savings in your 50s means you'll miss out on the most important retirement planning tool of all: time.

Spending Bow and Saving Later

This is another sign of procrastination.

"I adore when I get a pay increase, a promotion, or pay off debt! My financial flows have improved overnight!"

Remedy: Can You Handle a Market Recession as You Draw Closer to Retirement?

What should I do with the extra income flow each month when I see it improve? It should be the question you sit down and address with rigor and determination. For example, if you receive a 3% raise, you might consider increasing your retirement plan contribution by 1%. Then, you start a new job, earn a 10% rise, and enhance your retirement savings by 4%.

You pay off a $300 monthly auto loan; start by setting aside that money each month to create a down payment for the next car you buy. Increased cash flow is like a glass of red wine to the finances without using this discipline. Before you know it, your way of life has adjusted to the higher income, making changes more challenging.

Tomorrow's Syndrome

"Since you don't want to lose money, you invest cautiously. As a result, you might become more at ease with risk in the future"

Remedy:

Get comfortable with risk if you aren't in your younger years. You will need to save three to four times as much as you can—which is probably impossible. However, most of us will eventually need to make choices that call for blind faith and confidence, no matter how challenging that may be, taking the risk in exchange for a proportionate reward. A reasonable long-term expectation for the client, a well-allocated investor, is a 5%–6% return.

Counting on Your Parents or a Relative

"I'll receive an inheritance that will support me in my retirement."

Remedy:

I normally tell my clients to ignore potential inheritances. If it should happen, that's fantastic! But long-term care costs have wiped out many healthy nest accounts. For example, a $1 million portfolio could be depleted in as short as six to ten years by an 80-year-old patient who is admitted to the dementia section of a skilled care facility.

PROCRASTINATION AND PERSONAL FINANCES

According to a recent study, people who fear retirement more than death are the most likely to procrastinate on their retirement plans. The study was carried out by Boston College's Center for retirement persons. In the study, 1,000 persons between the ages of 50 and 70 were polled for Retirement Research. The researchers asked participants about their current work arrangements and found that those who fear retirement more than death were also most likely to have a plan in place for their final years.

But not every person who procrastinates on his or her retirement plan has reached this stage of life. Unfortunately, many investors never make it past the planning stage.

Why Do Investors Procrastinate on Their Retirement Plans?

If you're an investor who's procrastinating on your retirement plan, here are some reasons why:

You lack faith in your financial expertise and abilities. As a result, you may be afraid of making mistakes or being wrong about how much money you need for retirement—or even about whether or not you'll be able to retire in 20 years! If this is true for you, look over my seven steps for automating your finances today so that they'll be ready when the time comes, and you can focus on enjoying life instead of worrying.

You're a procrastinator, right? We all are. But are you also afraid of retirement? Is it as critical as death? If so, then you should take this section seriously. Your retirement savings is one of your biggest assets, and you better take good care of it!

Most people don't save for retirement because they don't understand the benefits of saving money. Instead, they think they're too young, don't have much time left in their lives, or simply don't feel like it today. Fear of retirement is one of the top reasons people don't save enough for retirement. And it's not just a fear of dying—it's also a fear of running out of money. But there's no need to worry about running out of money in retirement or dying.

FINANCIAL PLANNING FOR RETIREMENT: A PSYCHOSOCIAL PERSPECTIVE

Financial planning for retirement is a complex process. It involves understanding what you want, how much you can afford, and how to invest your money. The only person who can fully understand your circumstances is you. So, you've got a retirement plan in place; you've budgeted for it and started saving the maximum amount allowed. But have you ever given the psychological effects of retirement savings any thought?

Thus, the first step in financial planning for retirement should be determining why you want to retire and what that means. Then, once that has been established, it's time to evaluate where you stand right now and how much money you have already saved. This will help provide some context as you consider what changes need to be made to reach your goals. The next step is to develop an investment strategy based on these goals and needs—something that can be easily implemented using an appropriate tool like MS Excel or an online program like Money Manager Pro.

Once this is complete, it's time to examine each month's earnings and outgoings to find where there might be an opportunity for improvement in terms of increasing money savings or decreasing expenditure on pointless products. In addition, this analysis can help identify areas that need further attention, such as cutting down on taxes or increasing contributions toward retirement funds.

In actuality, retirement savings are about more than just money. It's also about self-esteem. It can be difficult to save for the future when you feel like you're not doing enough for yourself now—particularly if you don't have much savings or are just starting your career. That's why it's important to consider how your financial situation may affect your ability to save for retirement before jumping headlong into a plan.

The Mortality Paradox

A new study shows that people who plan for their retirement are less likely to die early than those who don't. The researchers studied more than 10,000 participants who were part of a large survey examining their health, financial status, and other factors. The participants were between 50 and 70 when they took the survey in 2008 and 2009. They were asked about their plans for retirement and how much they planned on saving for retirement.

Those who had a written plan were less likely to die early than those who didn't have a written plan or needed help with planning. In addition, those with a written plan with goals for retirement savings were also less likely to die early by about five years compared to those without a written plan or needing help with planning. That translates into an average savings of $10,000 over 15 years, starting at age 65 when you retire!

We all want to retire. But in actuality, most of us won't. Whether we have 30 or 30,000 years to live, retirement seems like a distant dream. Only about half of Americans who are eligible for Social Security receive it. And even those who receive benefits are not guaranteed they will get them; benefits are currently tied to annual inflation rates, which could decrease over time. Although there may be a significant difference between how people plan for retirement and how they live out their lives when they reach their golden years, strategies can help you be prepared for any eventuality.

Do You Fear Retirement More than Death?

Sometimes it is too late when people let fear prevent them from putting together a decent financial plan for their passing. We don't mean heights or sharks. Let's discuss the issues that genuinely terrify you the most as we work through your retirement fears.

- A lack of Funds

The largest worry, cited by 87% of respondents in Zety's research of more than 800 Americans, is not having enough money in retirement. It may involve anything from worrying that you'll need more money to having doubts about the Social Security program. For example, 32% of respondents indicated they were not confident that the government would pay out Social Security payments when they reached retirement age. A similar percentage thought the benefits would not be sufficient to support them.

- Physical & Mental Laziness

Most Americans were accustomed to a 9 to 5 job and a commute before the pandemic. People are used to being active, going for lunch, walking to meetings, and following a defined daily plan. One of the main worries about retirement is that you won't have this rigid routine anymore, and your thoughts won't always be focused on work. It's frightening to slow down—both psychologically and physically.

- Network for Work

Additionally, you might be concerned about your social life. Your social network is heavily influenced by the contacts you develop at work, so losing such interactions after you retire might be upsetting.

- Employment and Losing Health Benefits

Losing your employment-related health and medical benefits is also a significant determining element. One of the biggest worries is that we'll get sick and lose access to those benefits, especially as we get older and are more likely to require more medical attention. In this situation, people are concerned about having to pay medical expenses on a limited budget.

FINANCIAL ADVISORS' TOOL FOR EMOTIONAL INTELLIGENCE

Financial advisors are often tasked with helping clients manage their retirement plans. This can be challenging because people don't always know what they want and need from their retirement plan. The capacity to recognize, comprehend and control one's own emotions is known as emotional intelligence. Achieving emotional intelligence requires learning to read other people's emotions, interpret them correctly and respond appropriately to those feelings.

A financial advisor who has mastered this skill can help clients achieve their goals by understanding their emotions and motivating them to make the right decisions regarding their retirement plans.

Emotional Intelligence (EI) is a set of skills that help you understand and manage your own emotions and those of others. It's not just about being able to feel and express your emotions; it also means being able to understand them, manage them, and use this understanding in everyday situations.

In the workplace, EI can help you:

- Understand and manage other people's emotions.
- Resolve conflicts and maximize teamwork.
- Make choices that will benefit you and the company.
- Avoid costly mistakes in business decisions based on faulty assumptions or poor judgment.

Emotional Intelligence (EI) is the ability for you to recognize and manage your own emotions, as well as the emotions of others. It's a very important tool for financial advisors who want to build relationships with clients and understand how their emotions impact their decisions.

EI has a lot in common with the financial planning process itself. Financial advisors must understand and communicate with their clients, who may have different needs, preferences, and priorities. How do you use emotional intelligence in your work if you're a financial advisor? Here are five ways:

1) Listen actively – The most important aspect of EI is being an active listener. You need to hear what your client is saying, even if it's hard for you to understand. You also need to show that you care by paying attention, so they feel heard and understood.

2) Build rapport – Nothing builds trust faster than immediately establishing rapport with your client. Before you can

assist someone in achieving their objectives or resolving issues, you must build rapport.

3) Understand the sources of your stress – Analyze your stressors and take proactive steps to reduce them in your life. For example, leave it for the morning if you know that checking your work email right before night will send you into a tailspin. Leave it till you get to the office, if possible.

4) Recover from hardship – Everybody faces difficulties. Your response to these difficulties will determine whether you succeed or go into full-on meltdown mode. You are well aware of the power of positive thinking. Rather than moaning, try to be optimistic about assisting you to overcome hardship. What can you take away from this experience? Ask insightful questions to determine what you can learn.

5) Enhance your social skills – Emotional intelligence and social abilities frequently go hand in hand. Strong emotional intelligence makes it easier for one to read the feelings of others and respond appropriately. Improve your social skills by paying attention to nonverbal cues, actively listening, and actively seeking solutions when conflict develops.

The Importance of Emotional Intelligence in Relationships with Financial Planners

You don't have to be an expert in financial planning or investing to make a difference in the lives of others. Just be open to learning and trying new things. A recent study by the University of Pennsylvania found that emotional intelligence is important in financial planning relationships. The research also revealed that those with greater levels of emotional intelligence were more likely to establish trusting bonds with their clients, which eventually produced better results for all parties.

This is because emotional intelligence makes it possible for you to clearly convey what you can do for your client while also understanding their requirements and concerns. As a result, it helps you effectively communicate with clients, manage conflict, and handle difficult situations.

As a financial planner, you need to understand the importance of emotional intelligence in financial planning relationships to give your clients the best possible advice and guidance during their transition from working to retirement. Anyone who has ever had to plan for retirement has probably heard the same advice: "Do it now!"

The implication is that if you wait until later, you will be too late. But when it comes to retirement planning, the truth is that there is no magic formula for determining how long to wait before making a final decision.

The best approach is simply to start planning NOW.

That means taking your plans seriously and ensuring that you have all the information you need to make an informed decision about when you will retire. If you don't feel like taking this step right now, set up some future dates (such as three years away) as targets, and then write down your goals.

Once you have these things written down, sit down with a pen and paper and analyze all of the factors involved in your retirement plan: income sources, expenses, Social Security benefits, and so on. Again, keep this document as simple as possible so that it doesn't overwhelm you with numbers or other details that may cause confusion or distraction from your overall purpose.

If you're not doing your retirement plan right, you may want to consider getting the help of an independent financial advisor. An independent financial advisor (IFA) isn't a stockbroker or investment professional working for an insurance company, mutual fund, or other financial institution. Instead, an IFA is someone who is licensed to practice as an advisor in the state where he or she lives.

What you should understand before working with an IFA is as follows:

They have your best interests at heart. Many IFAs are former brokers or wealth managers who have decided that independent practice is their true calling. They are committed to their clients and will work hard for them, even if it means taking on extra work that's not part of their normal routine.

They are accustomed to working with various clientele. Many IFAs specialize in certain types of clients—for example, retirees, young families, or people with disability issues—so they can provide counsel specific to those needs. Some specialize in a particular industry, such as health care, but others focus more broadly on investing strategies and personal finance issues.

Financial planners are trained to provide unbiased advice, but emotions affect how clients perceive financial advisors. According to a study from the University of North Carolina at Chapel Hill, partnerships in financial planning lead to greater success when planners can use emotional intelligence skills and effectively manage their emotions.

Emotional intelligence is known as a person's capacity to recognize and comprehend their emotions, control and manage their emotions, and use emotional awareness to relate to others. According to the researchers, EI is important when it comes to helping people make sound decisions about money.

Financial planners who demonstrate higher levels of EI tend to have more satisfied clients and better performance outcomes, according to a research paper by Tracy Hanes-Mitchell, assistant professor at UNC's Kenan-Flagler Business School, Barbara Bradley-Cook, director at NC State's Center for Retirement Research, and Amy Finkelstein, director at Harvard Business School's Program on Negotiation and Dispute Resolution.

Here's an important question:

Why do some people procrastinate on their retirement plans while others don't?

The answer is complex and hard to pin down.

You may wonder if your age or health status affects whether or not you procrastinate on your retirement plan. Unfortunately, there's no definitive answer. But whether or not you put off saving for retirement seems to depend on a few different circumstances.

The Takeaways

- It's never too late to begin your retirement planning, regardless of your age or stage of life, and using the correct strategies now will make you look forward to retirement rather than fear it.
- Keep in mind that your golden years should feel vibrant and dazzling! By taking the appropriate actions early on, you may look forward to retirement and push yourself to earn it.

6

LIFE INSURANCE AND ANNUITIES

Life insurance and annuities are two important types of financial instruments you'll need to consider if you want to protect your family's future. Life insurance provides cash payments on your behalf at a specified future date or age. Payments can typically be made monthly, quarterly, semi-annually, or annually. Annuities provide lifetime income streams using a client's portfolio or existing assets. When people talk about annuities and life insurance, they are usually talking about the same thing. Life insurance is a life-coverage policy that provides financial security if you pass away before your debt is paid off. Annuities are just as they sound: annuity contracts pay out a specific amount of money over a period of time, based on how much you have already paid into an investment account. These may be in addition to your regular weekly or monthly payments, such as Social Security or pensions. Your purchase of an annuity will increase the total sum you have invested in your pension plan, with extra funds being automatically deducted from your bank or stock account. Let's look at ways you can make use of life insurance when planning to retire.

HOW TO USE LIFE INSURANCE WHEN PLANNING YOUR RETIREMENT

The importance of life insurance in a retirement income strategy is commonly undervalued. Consider insurance a safeguard for families if a breadwinner dies while at work. Financial advisors nevertheless advocate purchasing life insurance since it can be significantly more valuable when used properly in a thorough retirement income plan. To further understand how this functions, let's examine the four basic life insurance plans:

- Unit Linked Insurance/Plan (ULIP)
- Whole Life Plan
- Endowment Plan
- Retirement Plan

How to Use Life Insurance When Planning Your Retirement Unit Linked Insurance Plan (ULIP)

A ULIP is a product that combines investment and insurance. In addition to using your premium to cover your insurance life coverage, the insurance firm will invest any remaining funds in further investment options. Then, depending on how much risk you are ready to face with your investments, they will deploy the funds accordingly. They will allow you to invest in various things, such as debts, bonds, market funds, shares, and hybrid funds.

- Integrated Life Insurance

You are covered for the rest of your life or until you become 100. Your dependent will receive the capital if you pass away before the investment matures. After the period of premium payments expires under this plan, you can withdraw a portion of your investment or get regular cash.

- Endowment Plan

This long-term savings plan provides life insurance by using half of your premium. You will get a maturity or survival benefit from the insurance plan if life coverage continues for the duration of the endowment plan. The capital will go to your remaining dependent, such as your spouse, if the life insurance does not endure the entire term of the endowment plan. By choosing this option, you can occasionally earn extra money, which is paid to you at the end of the program or to the designated dependent in the event of your demise.

- Retirement Plan

Your retirement needs are catered for through a retirement plan. You can create a secure and cost-effective retirement plan using the retirement plan. The two phases of the retirement plan are accumulation and annuity.

- Accumulation Phase: The insurance company will ask you to pay your premiums during this phase's accumulation throughout the insurance plan's duration. Your premium payments to the insurance company will be used to purchase securities. In other words, they are investing the money you pay them, and over time, your investment will increase and bring in money for you.

Tips to Make Use of Life Insurance in Your Retirement Planning

- Select the right insurance coverage.

You must select the right life insurance coverage that checks all your boxes post-retirement. In addition, you must include retirement planning in your life insurance strategy if you want to benefit from it once you retire. Below are some suggestions on how to incorporate life insurance into your retirement planning so that you may make the best choice for you and your family:

- Include life insurance in your financial strategy.

Thanks to life insurance, your partner and children will be taken care of in case of your passing. You protect your family's and your future by including life insurance in your insurance strategy. You want the insurance plan payouts to pay off obligations and loans like your mortgage and car. Your dependents can use the money as they no longer depend on your income to pay for things such as their schooling. If your partner isn't employed, they'll need enough money to take care of the house and the kids. By choosing life insurance, people who die before retirement can still leave their families a financial legacy.

- The ideal way to save for retirement is through life insurance.

Life insurance provides financial security for your dependents if you pass away before you can save enough funds. Because life insurance has a low fixed cost, you can build an emergency fund because it increases your disposable income. In addition, you can start investing in low-cost investment options and buy long-term disability insurance.

- Timeframe of the Term

You will be asked to purchase a duration by the insurance company. You should consider your age and how long it will take you to save up enough money so that your dependents may live comfortably after you pass away before choosing the duration. For instance, if you are well above 65, you probably won't be eligible for the term.

- The recommended amount of life insurance.

How much debt you have already racked up, how much cash you will need to pay it off, and whether you have any responsibilities, like covering your child's college expenses, will determine how much life insurance you should get.

- Invest in Long-term Disability Insurance.

Do not rely on Social Security to cover your disability expenses. You will learn that it is difficult to qualify for Social Security benefits if you have a health condition that prevents you from working or if you have incurred an injury. Even if you do, the amount of money you will receive might not be enough to support your family. Long-term disability insurance should be a part of your retirement strategy. Own occupation coverage and any occupation coverage are the two available insurances. You should go for your occupation coverage because it will provide you with complete coverage. Your occupation insurance will restore your lost income if you cannot work in your field, such as accounting. The occupation coverage will restore your lost income if you cannot work in your industry, such as if you were an accountant instead of a retail worker. Applying for long-term disability insurance is necessary even if you are the sole person responsible for financial support. You will be paid enough to support your home even if you cannot work in your line of business.

- For retirement, use term life insurance.

For retirement, you need term life insurance. You must put the remaining funds into term life insurance to utilize it in your retirement plans. Although permanent life insurance is an option, you shouldn't invest the money directly through a brokerage house.

- Do not let your term life insurance policy expire.

If you have children, you get a term life insurance policy to cover them. However, the life insurance coverage expires when your kids grow up and leave the nest. Your insurance provider can advise you to replace your term life insurance policy with a new one to renew. Let your term life insurance policy lapse rather than replace it with another insurance plan. Save the money instead. Your partner can use your retirement, Social Security, and pension benefits to give them a consistent monthly income.

- Pay premiums with dividends.

You should utilize the coverage's dividends to pay down the payments if you wish to keep your previous whole life insurance policy so you can get tax-deferred income or when you pass away. You get an instant cash flow this way. In addition, you can grow tax-deferred with the dividends, and you get enough of them to cover your premiums.

- Your whole life policy can become a life annuity.

Your whole life insurance coverage must be changed to a life annuity. This can be accomplished by purchasing a life annuity with cash value. You won't have to pay much tax when you turn your complete life insurance policy into a life annuity. Before doing this, you should confirm with your insurance company if it is legal.

PLANNING FOR THE RETIREMENT YOU WANT AND ENVISION

How prepared are you? Hope you do not think it's too late already. When saving for a comfortable retirement, there is never a time too early or too late. Regardless of being in your retirement plan or how much you have to save for your life goals, you can still make plans to have a fun-filled, stressless, and more fulfilling life after retirement.

A retirement plan is in stages that evolve. To ensure you have a comfortable one, you must build a financial cushion to do the funding for you.

Making a retirement plan starts with your thinking. You think about your retirement goals and how long it will take you to achieve that. You should also consider the type of retirement account that will best assist you in raising the money you require after working. You know it is not about saving money for the future; you must be sure that the funds are invested to yield an increase and not just to be in your account. It is safer in an account where your money can grow.

The final part is taxes. Let's say you got tax deductions at the end of the year for the funds you have added to your retirement savings, then expect some amount to be paid as a tax bill when you withdraw your funds. However, there are ways you can save yourself from that stress. You can reduce the retirement tax hit while you save for your life after work.

You must consider all those issues you will learn about in this chapter. First, however, you must start with steps you should take to build a solid retirement plan. Your current age has nothing to do with this.

How many funds should you save?

Knowing how much you want to save shows you are preparing for retirement. This should be the first item on your retirement objectives list because you should have decided how much you want to invest for the future before you begin preparing. However, knowing the amount you plan to stash depends on many situational factors. For example, you need to consider your annual income and the age you plan to retire.

While no special rules guard the amount you can save, some financial advisors will tell you that saving up to $1 million is the best. Some will advise you to opt for savings that will span 12 years of your pre-retirement annual income. You might meet some retirement experts who will advise you to go for the 4% rule, which states that retirees shouldn't spend more than 4% of their retirement funds annually. Such advice is borne out of the fact that spending more than that could impair the comfortability you should enjoy after work. Since you don't have the same circumstances and opportunities that other people have, you need to take time to plan which one you will adopt. Such a plan is worth sitting down and calculating the best retirement saving option for your situation.

What you should consider

We have discussed the essentiality of making retirement plans and how much or what percentage of your income you want to splash into saving for the future. We must consider some pertinent factors or things you should consider when making such a plan. As you start contemplating retirement goals, it is worthwhile to consider some retirement impairments or challenges that can affect whichever plan you are making. For instance, you need to consider your family plans. For some people, starting a family is what they wish to do, but raising children can also cause a significant dent in your savings. Because of that, the kind of family you hope to have will be a major determining factor in your retirement plan.

You also need to think about your plans for life after work. For some people, changing their homes or moving to another apartment is their retirement plan. Many individuals would prefer to travel during retirement, and while that can be worth doing, an expensive journey will consume your retirement savings faster than you think. Traveling to less expensive places or staying at home might be the best option in such circumstances. Moving to a less expensive nation may allow you to stretch out your savings. A final note on that, you should consider the different options of tax-advantaged retirement accounts. Although most Americans enjoy Social Security, those benefits are too sparse to support all your needs after work.

Know the time you have

Your expected retirement age and current age create the groundwork for your retirement plan. The truth is that the longer the time you start saving, the higher the risk your portfolio can resist. If you are young and still have more than 30 years to work, you should consider having your assets in riskier investments. Something like stocks will be better. Though there will be volatility, stocks have been proven to be the best investment when considering the safety of your retirement funds. Remember, you are saving for an extended period, and when we talk about an extended period, we are talking about more than ten years of savings.

In addition to that, you need returns that can rise above inflation. That is necessary to ensure purchasing power during retirement. You should not risk saving funds and later discover that the value of your funds has reduced due to inflation. That can jeopardize your time in retirement. Do you remember how inflation starts, just like an acorn? Very little, but after some time, it turns into something bigger than what one can control.

Determine your post-retirement spending requirements

What are your post-retirement expectations? Having such knowledge will help you in no way in defining your portfolio size. For most people, post-retirement spending can only engulf 70% to 80% of their pre-retirement spending annually. But when you place that assumption side by side with actual reality, you will discover that they don't match—especially when you have not settled your mortgage.

Calculate your after-tax income

Once you've figured out your post-retirement spending and understand your time horizon, the next step is to calculate the amount you will have as your investment returns after you have paid your tax.

RETIREMENT ANNUITY

Consider a retirement annuity when you think of anything that can guarantee a lifetime income stream. This insurance package provides you with a steady income for retirement. One interesting thing about this package is that you can choose to enjoy it for your entire lifetime or a specific period.

In addition, your retirement annuity can be used alongside retirement savings and Social Security to create multiple financial sources when you are no longer receiving a paycheck. A retirement annuity is an insurance product that pays you a fixed income for life. You purchase an annuity from a financial institution or insurance agent who will keep buying the annuity for you until you die or until you decide to stop receiving payments.

When you buy an annuity, it's not just a one-time decision. Your current age is unrelated to this. The time you receive payments can vary depending on how much your current employer has contributed to your account and your age when you take out the policy.

If you want to buy a retirement annuity, you'll need to consider the following:

- Your age.
- Health and other criteria will determine how much you pay each month.

- What kind of policy will suit your needs? There are several types of annuities, including immediate-pay and deferred-payment policies. You can also choose between fixed-life or variable-life annuities, which have different tax implications
- How long do you want coverage? If you need more than three years of coverage, buying a long-term policy may be better than an immediate-pay policy.

Before we move into the significance and major drawbacks associated with retirement annuities, it's essential to know that they are not the same. There are a good number of annuities that you can choose from. However, four basic choices are based on two key decisions listed below:

Immediate vs. deferred annuities

With immediate annuities, you make a one-time payment that qualifies to start receiving regular payments immediately. This is usually good for older people. They just need to pay a huge sum for the annuity and start collecting payments once they hit the retirement period. This avails them of the opportunity to receive constant income after retirement.

On the contrary, deferred annuities are more appropriate for longer terms. After you make payment, you don't expect to receive any money until a specified date.

Variable vs. Fixed Annuities

You can subscribe to retirement annuities by making a single payment or in series. With the fixed annuities, you already know how much you will receive ahead of time after subscribing.

However, variable annuities don't work that way. Instead, your return is determined by the performance of your bond products and a basket of stocks you selected. But here, you enjoy bigger opportunities but at a greater risk.

Pros and Cons of Retirement Annuities

When it comes to the advantages and disadvantages of retirement annuities, there is much to discuss. First, however, let's look into them one after the other.

+ Pros

- Easier to Manage

Compared to other types of annuities, retirement annuities have several advantages. They are easier to understand and manage. Unlike some types of investment-based annuities, you do not need professional help when the time comes to decide whether or not a retirement annuity is right for you. You just need to know what questions to ask and what answers they'll give you. And while there may be some basic fees associated with this type of product (usually 1 percent per year), most people find them quite affordable compared to other types of annuities.

- Deferred Distributions

One benefit of annuities is their tax-deferred status. With numerous well-known retirement plans, such as CDs, payment is still expected to be made to Uncle Sam when they hit the maturity date. However, you don't have to bother paying the government any fees until you withdraw the money. Such an arrangement helps you as an owner to control your money after you pay your tax. In addition, you can reduce your Social Security taxes by operating a deferred annuity system. This is because your taxable income will be low by not withdrawing your money too early.

- Assured Rates

The amount you are paid from the variable annuities depends on the market performance. However, with the fixed type, you already know what your rate of return will eventually be.

— Cons

- Liquidity

One of the major concerns of retirement annuities is that it lacks liquidity. Most annuities come with what is known as a surrender fee, which restricts you from withdrawing your funds within the first few years of your engagement. Ordinarily, the surrender time covers 6 to 8 years of your investment. This charge is usually large, making it difficult to change your mind after the contract has been sealed.

- Hefty Charges

When you compare annuities' costs with CDs and mutual funds, you will discover that the plan is somewhat discouraging. The fact that some annuities are released through agents, whose commission can be extremely high with this kind of investment, dampens the advantages of the instrument.

Even if you decided to buy through a direct insurer, you could still face a sizable annual charge which is often 2% in excess. Sometimes, you could even pay more than that. Even if you take out special riders to reduce costs, you still expect to pay more.

Indexed annuities are similar to variable annuities, but they include a guarantee that your monthly payments will match the interest rate on a fixed-rate bond or another rate instrument for life. For example, 3% for life or 5% for life with a minimum payment guarantee.

The Takeaways

- Life insurance and annuities are two important types of financial instruments that you'll need to consider if you want to protect your family's future.
- Compared to other types of annuities, retirement annuities have several advantages. They are easier to understand and manage.
- The importance of life insurance in a retirement income strategy is commonly undervalued. Consider insurance a safeguard for families if a breadwinner dies while at work.
- With immediate annuities, you make a one-time payment that qualifies to start receiving regular payments immediately. This is usually good for older people.

7

MAKE SOCIAL SECURITY PART OF YOUR RETIREMENT

Including your Social Security benefits as a source of income in retirement is important and beneficial. Social Security has benefits and features that other savings plans do not have. Of course, planning diligently for your retirement years is vital because your welfare in your retirement years depends on how much you have planned. You must have had a few plans or certain plans you might be deliberating about taking on. There are different retirement plans in the United States with different perks and benefits. However, the benefit of Social Security is one of the benefits undermined by workers as a source of income in retirement. But we can never be entirely sure about the future, so it is better to be covered on all sides. Only 23% of workers say they have considered how to maximize their benefits in deciding when to claim Social Security, according to a survey in 2018 by the

Employee Benefit Research Institute, which is a significantly low portion of the population of workers. This chapter aims to sensitize you on the benefits of Social Security and why you should definitely consider it. If you have a retirement plan that considers your Social Security benefits, that is absolutely fine. You have definitely made a great choice that would ensure you are one step closer to ensuring that your assets last for the rest of your days. However, you should read about the benefits of Social Security that you may not have discovered.

SOCIAL SECURITY AND MEDICARE BASICS

For most individuals, Social Security is the bedrock of retirement income, and Medicare is likely your primary health coverage source. In this subsection, let's discuss when to claim Social Security and what Medicare is. To effectively prepare for retirement, you need to understand what Social Security benefits could do for you and how likely Medicare could be a primary source of health coverage. Understanding and knowing how and when to start taking advantage of these programs can help maximize your benefits, which will positively impact your welfare during your retirement years.

Who Can Claim Social Security Benefits?

You should be able to understand how Social Security benefits apply to your situation. Social Security is available for children, your spouse or former spouses, or people with disabilities. Suppose a loved one dies, such as a family member. In that case, some family members, such as widows or widowers, unmarried children, and dependent parents, may qualify for survivor benefits. However, qualifications may vary by dynamic situations; you should consult a financial consultant or a tax professional. There are a variety of Social Security benefits, but this is how to qualify for the retirement benefits that could make up a third of your monthly income.

You can claim this:

- If you are at least 62 years, which is the full retirement age, or older.
- If you have worked at least ten full years and your Social Security taxes were withheld, your ten full years do not need to be consecutive. You just have to have earned the "requisite 40 credits." You must have earned a certain number of credits in the US to qualify for Social Security benefits. The number of credits you need depends on your age when you apply and the type of benefit you are applying for. No one needs more than 40 credits for any type of Social Security benefit.
- If your spouse or ex-spouse worked for ten years or more and you qualify for benefits because of his or her work record.

When You Can Claim Social Security

Deciding what age to claim your Social Security benefits depends on you. As an American, you can file for Social Security as early as the age of 62. However, filing as early as 62 could significantly reduce the amount of money you could otherwise receive over your lifetime and the lifetime of a surviving spouse. In addition, if you are a woman, you must consider how early to claim your benefit as women tend to live longer and (as we mentioned earlier) earn less than men. Here are some reasons why timing is important:

1. Claiming Early

When you claim your benefits early, your benefits will be reduced by as much as 25% to 30%, depending on what year and date you were born. Suppose you are eligible for $1,000 a month at full retirement age; you could get $750 a month at age 62. However, the reduction will be less for every year you delay your filing between the age of 62 and your full retirement age.

2. Delaying Claiming

Suppose you wait to file for Social Security until after you have clocked your full retirement age. In that case, you can increase the size of your monthly benefits by a significant percentage, as much as 24% to 32%, depending on your full retirement age. However, after the age of 70, there will be no increase in the size of monthly benefits if you delay filing for benefits—no matter how long. Therefore, it would be rational to stop delaying after your 70th birthday. But, on the other hand, it wouldn't make sense to keep delaying benefits unless it is a tactic to save.

3. Your Full Retirement Age

According to the Social Security Administration, your full retirement age is the age you can claim your full retirement benefits from Social Security. It varies based on the year an individual is born. For people born between 1943 to 1954, it is 66, but it gradually increases to 67 for those born in 1960 or later. If you file for benefits before your full retirement age, your benefits would be drastically reduced.

Factors to Consider before Filing for Social Security Benefits

- Consider life expectancy. It refers to the number of years a person can expect to live; it is based on an estimated average age that members of a specific population will be when they die. Life expectancy relates to many medical and social factors, including career, race, genetics, gender, climate, medical and mental well-being, etc. For example, it was shown in a study that workers in the transport domain have the shortest life expectancy. Therefore, if you have any ailment or genetic disease that could impair or shorten your life expectancy, you should work toward having a retirement plan that serves you. You can also decide to file for your benefits earlier. However, delaying applying for your benefits is more beneficial if you have a longer life expectancy.

- If you are still working or have a business, you may not need to apply for your Social Security. However, constantly earning allows you to delay benefits and add more percentages to your benefits. This is why it is a rational decision to own a side business while working in a public or private organization.
- If you are looking to maximize your spouse's social benefits, for example, if you have a shorter life span than your spouse and desire to prepare for a financially secured future for them, then you can delay filing for benefits. If you die before your real retirement age, your benefits can still be transferred to your spouse. However, the qualification for this varies. You have to apply for a switch through the SSA-2 form only if you are 62 years and your spouse is not receiving Social Security benefits yet. It can also depend on your employment with the federal government, one of its states, or local subdivisions.

Three Strategies You Need to Know to Boost Your Social Security Benefits Before Filing

Delaying retirement:

Holding back the time to claim your Social Security benefits based on your work record is referred to as delayed retirement. You receive credits for every year you choose to wait past your full retirement age. This can be favorable if some factors exist in your financial situation, such as having your own business (see the previous subheading). Suppose an individual was born in 1943 or later. In such a case, one can increase their benefits by up to 8% per annum for each year they delay their claim to Social Security benefits. This applies to their full retirement age, up to age 70. After 70, there will no longer be added percentages. Note that you still need to sign up for Medicare at age 65 in case you need emergency coverage.

Filing and suspending of claim:

This strategy is pretty smart and immensely helpful. Individuals file for Social Security at full retirement age and then suspend their claim to accrue delayed retirement credits. This strategy used to be common among married couples but has been somewhat abandoned. However, if you are in one of the following situations, it is probably best if you apply this strategy:

- Suppose you file early for your Social Security retirement benefit before the full age of retirement and no longer need it. In that case, you can suspend the claim and still achieve an increase in the size of your monthly payments in the future, which can help offset some of the reduction to your benefit due to early filing.

- When your yearly income exceeds certain levels, a portion of your Social Security tax might be subject to income tax. If your income increases unexpectedly, suspending Social Security for that year could help significantly reduce your tax bill.

Restricted filing:

Individuals who are couples should approach the claiming of individual benefits separately as a team strategy. They can do this by using the advantage of both spousal and individual benefits as a way to maximize their income. One popular strategy for married couples filing for a spousal benefit is called spousal benefit with a restricted application. This strategy lets one spouse benefit from the other partner's records while still delaying their own Social Security benefits. However, since 2015, this strategy is no longer available to those born after January 2, 1954. A restricted application tells the Social Security office that you are not applying for all the benefits for which you are eligible at the same time. It simply involves the scope of your application. Therefore, your spouse could apply for a benefit that could cover both expenses, and you delay yours until it is financially mutually beneficial.

In the case of divorce:

If an individual is divorced from a person who is a worker and is entitled to a Social Security retirement benefit and your need at least 10 years, then you may also be entitled to claim benefits from your ex-spouse's record, even if they have remarried. An individual can receive spousal benefits on your ex-spouse's record if you are unmarried and are at least 62 years old. The benefit you are entitled to on your ex-spouse's record is more than what you could get through your own record. If an ex-spouse dies, as an ex-spouse, you may be entitled to a survivor's benefit on your dead spouse's record. You can also claim benefits as early as age 60 for reduced benefits or receive full benefits at your full retirement age. Another marriage does not have an impact on your eligibility after the age of 60.

Social Security benefits can be a vital supplement for retirement plans and contributions, and they can also help delay the liquidation of investments and to reduce tax costs. However, Social Security benefits can be taxed when your yearly income has reached a certain level. The more you make, the more of your Social Security benefits will be taxed. Make the best rational decisions you can make when it comes to filing.

How to Factor Social Security into Your Retirement Planning.

It is important to understand the key characteristics of Social Security while planning for a financially comfortable life after retirement. Understanding how the whole system functions is vital for your decision-making process.

- Social Security will be available when you retire: income taxes are one of the major funding sources for Social Security; the other two are trust funds and payroll taxes. Income tax makes up 89% of the program's total funding. This means that as long as individuals in the United States are working and paying their taxes, Social Security has a reliable influx of money. So there is absolutely no need to panic or be skeptical about considering Social Security benefits in your retirement plan.

- Social Security may be taxable. Your social benefits may be taxable based on how high your annual income is. If Social Security is your single source of income in retirement, then you do not have to pay taxes. But, if you receive income in addition to your benefits, such as receiving income from a traditional IRA, job earnings, or capital gains, your benefits may then be taxed. If a person files a federal tax return as an individual and your combined annual income is more than $34,000, up to 85% of your benefits may be taxable. A tax-deferred income source for Social Security purposes is qualified distributions from a Roth IRA that was contributed post-tax.
- Your benefits are based on a 35-year plan; it is based on your lifetime earnings, and adjustments are made for changes in average wages. The program bases your benefits on your 35 highest-earning working years. It is essential to review your status and ensure that your earnings are correct on the Social Security

Administration's website now that you are still planning.

- Your payout may be reduced. In 2019, there was a Social Security reserve of $2.9 trillion. However, the number of retired workers receiving Social Security benefits has increased from 33.5 million in 2009 to 45.1 million in 2019 and is growing at a steady rate every year. Reserves may be used up by 2035, but Social Security will not end; the payout will be significantly reduced. This is why it's vital to plan for supplementary financial retirement income.
- You will have to wait a bit longer for your full payout. People generally live longer and healthier in old age. The Social Security Administration raised the full retirement age to 67 for people born in 1960 or later. You can file for benefits as early as 62, although your benefit would be reduced by 30%. However, you can wait until the age of 70 to increase.

MEDICARE, BASICS AND BENEFITS

Medicare is a government health insurance program in the United States that subsidizes health care services for people aged 65 and older. An individual is qualified if such a person has paid payroll taxes and worked for at least ten years. It also covers younger people with specific eligibility criteria and some with specific diseases. There are different kinds of plans in Medicare that could cover an individual. It varies in healthcare situations; some may come at a cost to the insured individual. This presence of a variety of programs allows the program to offer consumers more choices but also makes it more complicated to get on the platform. Medicare will help with hospitalization costs and consultation with doctors as well. However, remember that you will need supplemental coverage to help pay for other healthcare-related expenses. It is vital to have profound knowledge about what is covered under the different parts of Medicare and how it suits your long-term plans and financial situation. Note that an individual has to be a United States citizen, a permanent legal resident (or married to one), and must have paid Social Security taxes for at least ten years to qualify for a Medicare plan.

So When Can You Claim Medicare Benefits?

Suppose you are not already receiving Social Security at 65. In that case, you must enroll for Medicare around your 65th birthday if you want to be able to access Medicare health coverage. Start the process three months earlier before you turn 65. Refusal to enroll before you are 65 may attract penalties, so do what you can to obtain substantial knowledge of enrollment deadlines and coverage options. When enrolled already, you can review and make changes to plans as time passes. However, you do not have to re-enroll each year.

How do you enroll in Medicare?

If you are not enrolled automatically, you should sign up for Medicare Parts A and B during the following periods:

1. Initial Enrollment Period: when you are initially eligible for Medicare, you have a time limit to sign up, which spans seven months and begins three months before your 65th birthday. It includes the month of your birthday and three months after your birthday.
2. General Enrollment Plan: if you miss the initial enrollment period, you still have the opportunity to sign up. You can sign up from January 1 to March of each year, after the year you reach your full retirement age. Then your coverage would begin on July 1. However, note that late enrollment in Medicare may incur penalties such as having to pay a higher premium.
3. Special Enrollment Period: if you or your spouse are currently working and covered by health insurance through an employer or union, then you will be entitled to a special enrollment period when such coverage ends. Suppose you have special disabilities and have a family member that is also covered by health insurance through an employer or union when such a family member's coverage ends.

The Types of Medicare Plans (A, B, and C)

Different options let you tailor Medicare to your needs. The Medicare Parts A and B plans are alternatively known as traditional Medicare. Parts C and D can increase the amount of your coverage or reduce costs. It is vital to know what kind of services each covers regarding your personal health needs. For example, some Medicare plans cover only limited dental, vision, and long-term care needs. So let's go through short descriptions of the basic costs and coverage provided by Medicare Parts A through D:

- **Part A:** This hospital coverage pays for in-patient hospital and nursing home care, home healthcare services, and hospice care. However, you must meet certain conditions to get these benefits. Most persons do not have to pay a monthly payment called a premium for Part A. This is because a spouse has paid Medicare taxes while they were working. If you didn't pay Medicare taxes while you have worked and are aged 65 or older, you might be able to buy Part A. There is an annual deductible, which is $1,556 in 2022. However, it is adjusted each year. An individual who has worked for at least ten years and paid payroll taxes qualifies for Part A Medicare.
- **Part B:** Part B medical coverage pays for doctor visits, routine exams, and other services and supplies not available under the coverage of Plan A. There is a monthly premium payment for Part B ($170.10 in

2022, or higher, depending on your income). It's typically deducted from Social Security benefits; an annual part of the plan is deductible, which is $233 per year in 2022. If you aren't already receiving Social Security, it will be charged to a person as a separate premium.

- **Part C** coverage can also be called Medicare advantage plans. These are federally approved policies that can be purchased from private insurers that are an alternative to traditional Medicare Parts A and B. Advantage plans offer, at minimum, the same coverage as offered under traditional Medicare plans.
- **Part D**, also known as drug coverage, is a Medicare plan that covers drug prescriptions federally approved and offered through private insurers. Some plans offer enhanced benefits and options. This type of Medicare plan is set up to share the cost of drugs until an individual reaches an annual limit. You can add part D coverage to traditional Medicare or a Part C Medicare advantage plan. However, some Medicare advantage plans already consist of prescription coverage. Monthly premiums vary by plan. However, enrolling as soon as you have reached full retirement age is more economical. If you don't, your premiums may increase, and you may still have to pay the penalty. There are two ways to get medical coverage in Plan D.

1. Medicare Drug Plans: These plans add drug coverage to your original Medicare, some Medicare Cost Plans, medical savings account plans, private fee-for-service plans, and medical Savings Account plans. You must have Medicare Part A or Medicare B to be eligible to join a separate Medicare drug plan.
2. You get all your Part A, Part B, and Medicare Advantage Plan through Medicare Advantage Plan (Part C) or Medicare Health Plan with drug coverage. However, not all these plans offer drug coverage. To join any Medicare drug plan or any Medicare health plan with drug coverage, you must be a United States citizen or be a legal permanent resident in the United States.

Social Security benefits are income and payouts you add to your retirement income plan. However, there may be some disadvantages, such as having to wait for seven years to reap full payouts. However, it can be a good supplemental income and help in emergencies. Medicare can also be very cost-effective regarding health care benefits and catering to your medical needs. Reading this chapter must have provided you with substantial information on filing for Social Security and enrolling in a Medicare plan and important rules and strategies to follow.

The Takeaways

- Do not shun Social Security benefits as a source of income in retirement; you need all the help you can get.
- Social Security is staying for a long time; payouts may be reduced, but be sure that Social Security benefits will still be available when you retire.
- Your Social Security benefits may still be taxed if you have a high source of income in retirement. But unless your Social Security benefit is the only source of income, then it may not be taxed.
- Use the specific strategies in this chapter to reduce tax costs and save, such as filing and suspending for Social Security benefits or delaying filing even when you have clocked full retirement age.
- It is always beneficial to enroll in Medicare as it can be cost-effective for health-related expenditures.

8

RETIREMENT BEYOND THE USA, THE UK AND CANADA

Making a retirement plan is not exclusive to Americans alone. Countries like the United Kingdom and Canada also have their retirement planning setting. And even in those countries, things are not the way they used to be. The workforce has been altered, lifestyles have changed, and many other things must be considered when retiring in the UK and Canada. For example, companies and retirement structures in Canada have taken a new form. Companies are now offering buyouts, and the life expectancy is now 85 years. Talk of inflation, goals, and aspirations have changed. So, you must take all these into consideration. It is equally advantageous as to what is obtainable in America, but as far as retirement is concerned, things can be different in other countries. For instance, the amount you need to stash into your retirement savings is not the same in the United Kingdom or Canada. Also, retirement plans designed and available for workers in Canada differ from those in America. Therefore, it's vital we consider this difference to see what is obtainable and available in a particular country as opposed to another.

Let's consider the Canadian retirement plan:

CANADA RETIREMENT PLANNING

In Canada, there are different types of retirement income and saving plans. According to a survey done by the Canadian Imperial Bank of Commerce (CIBC), every Canadian needs a total estimation of $756,000 as personal savings to have a comfortable life after work. But unfortunately, more than 90% of Canadians don't have a plan to accomplish this.

Below are the steps one needs to take to achieve a retirement plan in Canada:

Decide how much you need for retirement.

Knowing the exact amount you want to save is the first step when planning your after-work life. And under this, you need to:

- Set your after-work goals—knowing and having a list of what you want to achieve in your after-work life.

- Make some comparison between your current spending with your future spending.
- Decide when you start the journey—decide on when to start resting.
- Make plans for unexpected expenses during after-work life.
- Think about possible inflation and after-work realities.

Let's break it down for better understanding.

Set your after-work goals.

The amount you are going to save depends on how much you will need during retirement. And to know how much you will actually need; you need to consider the following:

- Your interests/hobbies.
- Retirement age.
- The decision whether to work after retirement. Perhaps as a consultant.
- If you've grown up with children and grandchildren, who will be willing to help?
- Where will you live?
- Your travel plans—are there going to be vacations?
- Do you have debts to pay, such as loans or mortgages?

Current spending vs. expected retirement spending; make a comparison.

Take a look at what you are spending money on now. Then, check if there will be changes after you retire. Definitely, there will be. For instance, you won't need to spend money to get to work. You won't need money to buy lunch at work or attend to anything regarding work that engulfs money. Notwithstanding, expenses, such as traveling, medical, and other expenses, are almost inevitable.

Moreover, consider discounts on goods and services you want to purchase. In Canada, many businesses offer discount charges for seniors who patronize them on a wide range of goods and services, ranging from public transportation, education, entertainment and travel, and household supplies or groceries.

So, when you visit those places, always remember to ask for seniors' discounts. That could save you a whole lot of money.

Decide when you are ready for the journey.

Knowing when you are going to reture dramatically impacts how much you need to save for your retirement. It's vital to have basic knowledge of when you are expected to retire. You are not going to work forever. So you need to ensure you have enough money to assist yourself in coping with retirement expenses and spending.

- When you are thinking about that, think about the following:
- The kind of life you want after work.
- Your spouse's retirement plans.
- Your current financial observations.
- The amount you will be receiving as pensions, personal savings, and investments.

Your life expectancy also influences how much you have to save for retirement. It's noteworthy that today's Canadians live longer than past generations. So be smart enough to budget for more than 30 years of life after work.

Make plans for unexpected expenses during after-work life.

Unprepared or unexpected events have a significant influence on your retirement savings. It's possible you could encounter:

1. The need to retire because of age factors, professional, personal, or health reasons.
2. Unplanned expenses such as a car or home repairs.
3. The need to change your home because of a change in your health or that of a beloved person.

To achieve any of these things successfully, you need to set up an entirely different savings tool or type of investment to use as an emergency fund. For example, you can earmark a certain percentage of your income and deposit it into your retirement account. That sum is enough for you to rely on for the next 3 to 6 months.

Think about possible inflation and after-work realities.

In Canada, inflation is a big deal. It is calculated using the consumer price index. CPI is a tracker that is used to track how the price of over 600 consumer goods and services of Canadians changes within a period of time. Recently, it's just 2% per year. That means the cost of commodities has been rising by 2% yearly.

This, however, can influence the amount you are saving for retirement and your future plan. But you can still rely on the amount you get from the Canada Pension Plan and Old Age Security to help rescue you during hard times.

Budgeting during Retirement in Canada

Budgeting is not only a wise step you take when you are working; it's a practice you engage in even when you are no longer receiving any paycheck. Though your budget—while you are working—will be different from your budget when you are not working, you still need to ensure you are not just spending money on things you want and not on things you need. For instance, you will probably spend less on going to work, but you are going to spend more on traveling. Also, how you spend money during the early stages of your retirement will be different from how you will allocate it after a long period of retirement. For example, you can spend more on housing because you may need to move to a seniors' apartment for comfort.

You must learn how to track, review, and update your budget regularly. What you get from a pension may not be the same every time. You can leverage the Canadian Retirement Income Calculator to figure out what your retirement income will likely be.

Retirement in Canada vs. America: Are There Any Differences?

When it comes to retirement plans, Canada and America offer similar services. However, Canadians find life after work less stressful as the fear of losing money is not as common as in the US. The fear of running out of money has forced many Americans to use diverse means to supplement their retirement incomes.

One of the major benefits that Canadian retirees are enjoying is the universal healthcare system that is publicly funded. This system allows them to enjoy essential medical services throughout their lives without any copay or deductibles, whereas there are no such plans in the United States. In fact, unless you are disabled or have an extremely low income, there is nothing like a single-payer insurance scheme for you until you reach the age of 65. In the United States, age 65 qualifies them for Medicare. Yet, we can't truly say that that is comprehensive enough for people who have worked for years because the system covers only 62% of the entire healthcare costs.

Major Differences

When it comes to saving for life after work, both countries offer similar and advantageous financial vehicles and tax advantages.

RRSP vs. Traditional IRA and 401(k)

Canadian retirees have the privilege to enjoy tax deductions with the operation of Registered Retirement Savings Plans. The sum of money splashed into savings grows tax-deferred, enhancing the compound returns' benefits. You can still make contributions until you reach the age of 71. The government is responsible for setting the maximum limits on the amount you can have in the RRSP account.

According to the Canada Revenue Agency, the RRSP increases from $27,890 for 2021 to $29,210 in 2022. This allows investors to make more contributions; even the addition of more than $2,000 may attract liable penalties.

Traditional IRAs

In America, you can make limited contributions compared to Canada. The maximum contributions set for traditional IRAs are at $6,000 per year for both 2022 and 2021, or the amount of your taxable income for that financial year. That allows people above the age of 50 to sock away an additional $1,000 per year in 2021 and 2022 as a catch-up contribution.

America's Roth IRA vs. Canada's TFSA

America's Roth IRA is fairly similar to Canada's Tax-Free Savings Account. However, both of them are funded from the leftover money after you have paid your tax. That means there will not be a tax deduction in the year such contribution is made. However, holders of both accounts enjoy tax-free earnings growth. They are also not taxed when they make a withdrawal.

Social Security

The American Social Security structure is not only tailored toward the welfare of retirees but also to other additional areas, such as Medicare, disability income, and survivor benefits. In addition, the Social Security structure is more complex because it hinges on several factors, such as whether or not the recipient's income is generated through other means, information gathered on the IRS from SSA-1099, and the recipient's marital status.

AMERICA VS. THE UNITED KINGDOM

No one would say the cost of living in the United Kingdom is relatively fair, but it is a bargain compared to the high cost of living in New York City. You will need nothing less than $4,700 per month to live a modest lifestyle in the capital of the United Kingdom, compared to over $5,000 per month in the US.

An agreement between the United Kingdom and the United States was designed to improve Social Security protection for the workforce in both countries. This arrangement helps many disabled and monthly retirees who are not under any country's Social Security system. This provision became effective in January 1988, which is primarily for countries like England and Northern Ireland.

However, this does not cover benefits under the US Medicare program or the supplemental security income program.

How to Retire Early in the UK – the FIRE Method

If you plan to retire in the UK, you have probably heard of the FIRE (Financial Independence Retire Early) method. It is a popular way to retire early and live on a fixed income until age 65 or 70.

The FIRE Method is an acronym for four financial principles:

1) Frugality: Making sure you live below your means (so that your lifestyle doesn't change much as you get older).

2) Investing: Having enough savings in a retirement account to live comfortably when you stop working.

3) Index Funds: Investing in low-cost index funds that track broad market indexes, such as S&P 500 or MSCI World Indexes.

4) Reach for Roth: Using tax-advantaged accounts like 401(k)s, IRAs, etc., instead of taxable accounts.

The FIRE method is based on the idea that if you can save enough money for retirement, you can live off it for the rest of your life. So, if you can save $1 million by age 30, it works out that retirement will require only about $300 per month from Social Security and other sources like pensions. This sounds great until you realize that Americans spend more than $1,200 monthly on housing costs alone! And if you want to own a home, even after paying all those expenses, you may not be able to afford your monthly living expenses. The point is that saving enough for retirement doesn't necessarily equate with living comfortably during retirement. This is because there will still be many expenses associated with owning property and other things you need to purchase when folks are still working. Things like cars, furniture, appliances, and clothing. So, what's the solution? How do we save enough money? Is it possible to retire at 40? Let's take a look at it below.

It's possible . . . but it's not easy. It takes a lot of money, and you must be very disciplined about saving. If you're not willing to put in the time and effort, then don't even try. To retire at 40, you need to have a high income and low expenses. Your income should be somewhere between $100,000 and $200,000 per year. Your expenses should be less than half of that amount. If you're making more than

$200,000 annually, you should probably be working for someone else to retire comfortably without having to work.

What Are the Steps to Retire Early?

If you're wondering how to retire early, there's a lot to think about. Here are some steps to retire early that can help you to work out your strategies:

Save

Most people who save for retirement save 25% to 50% of their monthly salary. You may need to make some lifestyle adjustments and identify necessary expenses to save this money. Consider implementing these budgeting tips.

Additionally, you must choose where to invest your savings. Most FIRE savers will invest in an ISA (individual savings account) or another tax-efficient vehicle through stocks and shares.

Spend Wisely

Before making any purchases, give it some thought. Many save money, eschew buying luxuries and find other ways to acquire things. That might entail giving up your morning coffee habit and staying away from sandwiches. Instead, you may use your savings to increase your investments or pay off your mortgage more quickly.

Should I Open a Pension, ISA, or Both?

If you're over 60, you can open a pension and have it invested in a government-backed fund. This means it will be guaranteed by the state and paid out whenever you retire. If you're under 60, there's no guarantee that your pension will pay out when you retire. But if it doesn't, the government would make up the difference between what you have left and what they pay out to anyone else who has retired earlier than you. So pensions are best for people of all ages; they might not be as good as ISAs, but they're still better than nothing.

FINANCIAL RESILIENCE

Financial resilience is the ability to maintain a standard of living after retirement. This might mean that you continue to live in the same home or make your money last for several years longer than usual. Financial resilience depends on how much you have saved and how old you are when you stop working. If you have worked steadily for many years, your savings can be used to support your retirement lifestyle in many ways, even if you can only continue working for a few years. On the other hand, if you have saved little or nothing for retirement, it may be difficult to maintain your lifestyle because of changes in your income and expenses. The challenge is greater if you move from one job to another and lose access to employer-provided benefits such as health care coverage, pensions, or retirement plans. Financial resilience is not something you can turn on and off like a switch—you either have it or you don't. When you are financially resilient, you will be able to make sound financial decisions regardless of what is going on instead of reacting to stressful situations that may not be as big of an issue as they seem at the time (like when your rent is late). Financial resilience also means handling unexpected expenses without getting into debt or losing sleep because you know that if things go wrong, there's always something else that can be done until things get back on track again.

If you want to be financially resilient, here are some things that can help:

1. Develop an emergency fund of six months' worth of living expenses in case of an unexpected job loss, illness, or accident.

2. Pay off your credit card balance monthly with the highest interest rate first and only use cash advances for emergencies such as car repairs or medical bills.

3. Set up automatic monthly transfers from your checking account into savings each month so that money isn't sitting idle in an account earning anything but interest charges while it can earn interest elsewhere.

The Takeaways

- Financial resilience is the ability to maintain a standard of living after retirement. This might mean that you continue to live in the same home or make your money last for several years longer than usual.

- The FIRE Method is an acronym for four financial principles:

Financial
Independence
Retire
Early

- Frugality: Making sure you live below your means (so that your lifestyle doesn't change much as you get older).
- Investing: Having enough savings in a retirement account to live comfortably when you stop working.
- Index Funds: Investing in low-cost index funds that track broad market indexes, such as S&P 500 or MSCI World Indexes.
- Reach for Roth: Using tax-advantaged accounts like 401(k)s, IRAs, etc., instead of taxable accounts.
- If you're over 60, you can open a pension and have it invested in a government-backed fund. This means it will be guaranteed by the state and paid out whenever you retire.

CONCLUSION

So, how do you feel about your retirement plan? Do you have a clear picture of what it should look like? You've read the entire book and learned all about setting your financial goals. You're ready to take action! Great! Now that you know how to set your financial goals, it's time to take action and make those plans a reality. There are many different ways to go about this, but one thing is certain: retirement planning is not something that happens overnight.

You've worked hard for your retirement, so you owe it to yourself to enjoy it to the fullest. Don't be frightened to pursue your goals in life and to have great dreams. Make sure you live your life the way you want to since it is your life. And don't look back. Fear has a way of stealing our dreams. We allow our inner critic to keep us from achieving our goals.

To sum up, financial planning for retirement is all about taking care of your future. It's about knowing what you need to do and when, and it's not always easy. But it's worth it—and you can do it!

If you want to be confident that you have a solid plan set in stone, then you need to start now. Don't wait until tomorrow—start today!

RESOURCES

AARP(2022), How is Social Security Funded, AARP, retrieved from https://www.aarp.org/retirement/social-security/questions-answers/how-is-social-security-funded.html, Accessed on 15th, 2022.

Benjamin (2020) "How the Gender Income Gap Impacts Women's Retirement" https://www.forbes.com/advisor/retirement/retirement-gender-income-gap/. Accessed on 2nd August 2022.

Bryson (2019). "How to Use Emotional Intelligence in the Workplace" Retrieved from https://www.bamboohr.com/blog/emotional-intelligence-workplace. Accessed on 12th August 2022.

Glenn (2008). "Retirement Planning - The Cost of Waiting" Retrieved from http://EzineArticles.com/2158542. Accessed on 12th August 2022.

Global Partnership for Financial Inclusion (GPFI) (2019) %20Aging%20and%20Financial%20Inclusion.pdf. Accessed on 1st August 2022.

HHS.gov, (2022). "What is Medicare Part A?" retrieved from https://www.hhs.gov/answers/medicare-and-medicaid/what-is-medicare-part-a./index.html#

Megan et. al (2013) "Narrative Financial Therapy: Integrating a Financial Planning Approach with Therapeutic Theory" Vol 4 retrieved from https://newprairiepress.org/cgi/viewcontent.cgi?article=1052&context=jft. Accessed on 29th july 2022.

Michelle Fox, (2021) Retrieved from "Don't let fear and anxiety ruin your financial life. These strategies can help you stay on track" How to prevent fear and anxiety from ruining your financial life (cnbc.com). Accessed on 2nd, August 2021.

Mind, (2021) "The link between money and mental health" Retrieved from https://www.mind.org.uk/information-support/tips-for-everyday-living/money-and-mental-health/the-link-between-money-and-mental-health/. Accessed on 2nd, August 2022.

Nathan (2022) "How Financial Therapy Can Lead to a Brighter Financial Future" retrieved from https://www.moneygeek.com/financial-planning/what-is-financial-therapy/.Accessed 29th July 2022.

Nicholas (2021). "Emotional Intelligence – A Tool for Financial Advisors" Retrieved from https://www.im.natixis.com/us/portfolio-construction/emotional-intelligence-a-financial-advisors-tool.Accessed on 12th August 2022.

Queen (2021) "Aging and Financial Inclusion" https://www.gpfi.org/sites/gpfi/files/documents/G20%20Fukuoka%20Policy%20Priorities%20on. Accessed on 12th August 2022

World Health Organization (2021) "Ageing and health" retrieved from https://www.who.int/news-room/fact-sheets/detail/ageing-and-health. Accessed on 1st August 2022.

Zoe (2022). "Do You Fear Retirement More Than Death?" Retrieved from https://zoefin.com/learn/investors/fear-retirement-more-than-death/. Accessed on 12th August 2022.

Made in the USA
Monee, IL
04 November 2026

67386997R00095